WILLIS

A Short History

WILLIS

A Short History

MICHAEL CLAYDON

Haggerston Press

Copies may be ordered from:

Michael Claydon

31 Marville Road

London SW6 7BB

michael.claydon@hotmail.com

Price: £15

£20 including UK p+p

Frontispiece: The Willis Building in Lime Street
© Stanhope by Hufton + Crow 7

First published 2012 by Haggerston Press,
38 Kensington Place, London W8 7PR
Printed in Great Britain by Martins of Berwick

ISBN 978 1 869812 27 0

Contents

Illustrations

In grateful memory of my mother and father

MAY AND STANLEY CLAYDON

Preface

I joined Willis Faber & Dumas Limited in October 1962. It was privately owned, with members of the founding families actively engaged in its management. There were, as I recall, around 800 employees across two offices in Leadenhall Street and an out-of-town office at Westcliff in Essex. There were also branch offices in Birmingham, Bristol, Cardiff, Sheffield and Warrington. When I retired in July 2010, Willis Group Holdings had 25,000 employees around the world, its shares were quoted on the New York Stock Exchange and it had a market capitalisation of over $5 billion.

In my retirement speech I gave a personal reminiscence of my long career and briefly described some of the outstanding men who had built a proud and great firm, a firm that was in business nine years before Victoria came to the throne. It struck me that most of the audience had scant knowledge of its history. A number of people were kind enough to suggest that I should write something about that history. In doing so, I have drawn heavily upon the meticulous research of Digby Brindle-Wood-Williams, who in 1982 was commissioned by David Palmer, then Chairman, to write a history of the first one hundred years of the firm. This was never published.

I have tried to tell a story of remarkable men, remarkable events and a remarkable firm. This is neither a definitive history nor an authorised one. It is, rather, a brief account of a firm I was privileged to serve for almost fifty years.

The Chairmen

There have been only fifteen Chairmen in the long history of the firm.

Henry Willis	1828–82
David Willis	1882–1911
Arthur Allan	1911–34
George Stamp	1934–37
Henry Willis	1938–47
Raymond Dumas	1947–54
Elwyn Rhys	1955–65
Derek Ripley	1966–67
John Roscoe	1967–71
Julian Faber	1972–77
Ronnie Taylor	1978–81
David Palmer	1982–88
Roger Elliott	1988–95
John Reeve	1995–2000
Joe Plumeri	2000–present

The Families

The history of Willis is inextricably bound up with three families: those of Willis, Faber and Dumas. They started the firms which laid the foundations of what, today, is Willis Group Holdings.

WILLIS

Henry Willis (1800–82) was born on 21 July 1800, the third son of David and Ann Willis. His father was a prosperous farmer at Cobham in Surrey. The family had settled at Long Ditton in the same county in the early part of the seventeenth century, and over the years had acquired land at nearby Kingston, Molesey and Cobham, as well as at more distant Staines.

FABER

While the Fabers were active in insurance in the Victorian era they did not go into business as Faber Brothers until 1888. George Henry Smith (1799–1895) could be called the founder of the firm, as he is the first traceable member of the family to appear on the Lloyd's Roll, in 1863, as an Underwriting Member. He was then living in East Dulwich; originally the family came from County Durham. Three of his sons – George (1839–1910), Alfred (1851–1931) and Walter (1856–1932) – had changed their surname by deed poll from Smith to Faber in 1886 (*Faber* in Latin can mean smith, as in blacksmith).

DUMAS

The Dumas family was altogether more exotic, and had a much longer connection with insurance than either Willis or Faber.

The Families

Most of the Dumas family were staunch Huguenots who would have suffered persecution after the Revocation of the Edict of Nantes in 1685. What is known is that one member of the family, Jean Dumas (1654–1720), fled France with his wife and children in 1689. They ended up in the French Protestant colony in Hamburg – then an independent free city and one of the greatest ports of Europe, prosperous since the creation of the Hanseatic League in the thirteenth century. Jean Dumas' second son, Jean-Pierre (1687–1745), started a cutlery business which continued through to his grandson, also Jean-Pierre (1764–1840), expanding into the manufacture of surgical instruments. In 1800 the second Jean-Pierre gave up his Hamburg business and established himself in Paris. He had three sons and three daughters. His eldest son, Henri (1794–1843), left the family in Paris and came to London soon after the end of the Napoleonic wars, where he joined Barings Bank.

CHAPTER ONE

—➤•●•◄—

The Nineteenth Century

Being born the third son, Henry Willis had to leave the farming to his two older brothers and seek a career elsewhere. In 1820 he was apprenticed to a partner in the firm of Garry E. Curtis, who were merchants engaged in importing grain and wheat from North America. After eight years Henry went into business on his own account as a commission merchant, establishing himself initially at the Baltic Coffee House, then later in Threadneedle Street. The Coffee House was a direct precursor of the Baltic Exchange, a place where cargoes for merchant ships could be arranged. Today this activity is known as freight chartering.

A commission merchant worked very much like a present-day import agent, selling a variety of commodities on commission to customers in the United Kingdom on behalf of overseas produ-cers. Henry Willis traded in a large range, including flax, linseed, tallow, grain, skins, oats, wheat and timber. These were imported into England principally from ports in the Baltic, and East Prus-sia in particular, where Henry made agency agreements with shippers. From the Baltic Coffee House he established a customer base in towns and cities throughout the United Kingdom. Once an introduction had been made, Henry would then set about checking his prospective client's credentials, making enquiries through banks, brokers and other merchants. Today we would call this 'due diligence', or more simply, 'know your customer'. While no financial records appear to survive for this period it is

Henry Willis, founder of Henry Willis & Company

clear that the business prospered. The industrialisation of the United Kingdom created a huge demand for raw materials, and deregulation, in the form of the repeal of both the Corn Laws and the Navigation Acts, ushered in an era of free trade. Around 1839 Henry started doing business with the United States, handling incoming cargoes of wheat, flour, cotton, fruit and dairy products, and outgoing shipments of Russian bristles for brush manufacturers in New York. He had also developed some export trade which included sending Cornish tin to St Petersburg.

It would seem that as early as 1835 Henry had involved himself with insurance. In 1841 he applied for membership of Lloyd's, where initially he broked the cargoes of those commodi-

16

ties which he sold on commission. Through the 1850s and 1860s the brok-ing side became less dependent on the commission business as Willis obtained many clients throughout the United Kingdom, particularly from Liverpool and Leeds, for whom he arranged cargo insurance. Whilst cargo was the mainstay of the insurance broking activity, Willis also became involved in hull business, probably around 1865.

In 1840 the firm moved, firstly to 37 Old Broad Street and then to 30 Great Winchester Street, where it remained until 1866, before returning to various addresses in Old Broad Street. In 1879 the commission agents' business was sold to the management and the firm moved to South Sea House in Threadneedle Street. Following Henry's death, the firm finally settled in 32 Cornhill in 1888. By this time, the firm was styled Henry Willis & Company. Because Henry's marriage had been childless, he took David and Thomas, the sons of his oldest brother David, into the firm.

In 1873 a 14-year-old boy named Edwin John Spencer joined the firm as a junior clerk earning £20 a year. His subsequent contribution to the firm until his retirement was quite remarkable. In his memoirs, *Recollections of my Business Life*, Spencer painted this splendid portrait of the firm he joined:

The partners were Henry Willis, age 72, and his nephew, David Willis, age 34. Henry Willis was rather a picturesque personality; of a spare and comparatively upright figure above medium height, with regular features, rosy cheeks and snow-white side whiskers; dressed in a swallow-tail coat, light vest and shepherd's plaid trousers, a stock round his throat and a bright flower in his button-hole, and a light beaver tall hat in summer, but a black one in winter. He only came to the office once or twice a week, and his authority was abso-lute; he had shrewd, clear ideas and a very proper sense of justice, but he also had extremely strong prejudices.

He denounced drinking and smoking, forbade the wearing of a moustache, urged the wearing of a stock, demanded that everyone should speak audibly and clearly, and declared that steel instead of quill pens, railways and telegraphs were the curse of the age. What was of most importance, however, was that he had some peculiar views in regard to the business.

David Willis was tall and spare, with pale, delicate features, fair hair, and long side-whiskers; and he always wore a frock coat, black bow tie, and dark trousers. He was not only of a naturally retiring disposition, but he systematically kept himself in the background, although he had most excellent intelligence together with the highest principles, and in those days worked most assiduously.

The staff consisted of the manager, David Black, aged 35, and four other clerks besides myself. The offices were two rooms and a small room for samples on the top floor of an old house, 20 Old Broad Street, London, long since pulled down, and the rental was £80 a year. The hours were nominally from 9 a.m. till 6 p.m., but the clerks never left the office by 6 p.m., and sometimes not before 9 p.m. and 10 p.m. They got a very occasional half-holiday on Saturday, and a fortnight's holiday in the summer; Bank holidays had not then been instituted. David Black led the buyout of the commission agents' business in 1879. It appears that the decision was made because of an increasing requirement by their principals to take a direct financial interest in the commodities they handled and not merely take a commission on the transaction.

Henry Willis died in 1882, leaving David Willis as the only partner in the firm until Edwin Spencer became one in 1886. Henry Willis had insisted that the firm should engage in insurance broking only, and that underwriting and reinsurance, respectively the acceptance and laying off of risk, were to be avoided. This was irksome to Edwin Spencer, who believed them to be a natural adjunct to insurance broking. He now set about develop-

David Willis

ing these with great energy, and by the end of 1882 had obtained the underwriting agency for the Italia Company of Genoa. This was followed by agencies from the Sea Company of Liverpool, four European companies (Assicurazioni Generali of Trieste, the Oberrheinsche, the Leipziger and the Commerz) and the United States Lloyd's. All the underwriting activity, which was undertaken from 32 Cornhill, was conducted alongside insurance broking, which continued to be the principal activity of Henry Willis & Company.

Building the underwriting business was by no means Edwin Spencer's only contribution to the company. Willis were placing business for the New York brokerage Wreaks & Chubb. Thomas

Edwin John Spencer

C. Chubb withdrew from the broking firm to concentrate on underwriting and with his son Percy formed Chubb & Son. The broking firm became Wreaks & Loines. In 1891, after Wreaks's death, the firm was absorbed into Johnson & Higgins, and Stephen Loines joined them. Johnson & Higgins of New York were the largest hull broker in the United States. They had started life in New York in 1845 as Jones & Johnson, average adjusters and marine insurance brokers. This partnership was dissolved, and in 1854 the firm was renamed Johnson & Higgins. Their correspondents in the United Kingdom were John D. Tyson of Liverpool, whose London agent was George Tyser.

As a result of a brilliant broking coup involving the American

Line and engineered by Spencer and Loines, Johnson & Higgins started giving business to Henry Willis & Company. The relationship developed in 1892 when two Partners of Johnson & Higgins, Loines and John D. Barratt sailed to Southampton to meet David Willis and Edwin Spencer. This led to Henry Willis & Company gaining a larger share of Johnson & Higgins's business. The relationship was put on a more formal footing in 1896.

Rather less is known about Faber Brothers. As noted earlier, the first traceable member of the family to appear on the Lloyd's Roll as an Underwriting Member is George Henry Smith. By 1864, George Henry Smith Junior is recorded as trading on his own account as an insurance broker and shipping agent. He had an office at 1 Great Tower Street, where he remained until 1893, when he moved to 11/12 St Clements Lane, Lombard Street. In 1886 the Smiths changed their name to Faber. This was the same year that George and his brother Alfred formed Faber Brothers and the latter was brought into the Partnership. The third brother, Walter, had joined George and Alfred at Lloyd's in 1883, but for reasons unknown, he never became a Partner of Faber Brothers.

Hubert Langrish Faber, George's son, joined Faber Brothers in 1893 and, from the beginning, concentrated on the underwriting side of the firm. He became a Partner in 1897. Around the same time a young man, not of the Faber family, had joined the firm and been taken into Partnership. His name was Arthur Campbell Allan and his father had been Speaker of the Canadian Parliament. Arthur Allan's influence on Willis Faber was to rival that of Edwin Spencer.

On 1 January 1898 Henry Willis & Company merged with Faber Brothers to form the newly registered Willis, Faber & Co. Limited. The Directors were David Willis (Chairman), Edwin John Spencer, Henry Willis, David Willis Jnr, George Henry

Faber, Alfred Faber, Arthur Campbell Allan and Hubert Langrish Faber. Edwin Spencer claimed in his memoirs to have instigated the merger discussions with George Faber as Senior Partner of Faber Brothers, the rationale being that Faber Brothers had stronger relationships at Lloyd's than did Henry Willis & Company. A dinner was held at the Savoy to celebrate the event, at which the speeches addressed concerns that the new firm would be 'too strong a combination, a menace to competitors and the market'.

The Company's capital was set at £125,000 made up of 1,250 shares of £100 each. Of these, 1,000 shares were to be issued (£60 per share paid up) and divided equally between the Willis and Faber Directors. The allocation of 1,000 shares was as follows:

David Willis	150	(originally 250, but he gifted 50 to both Henry and David Jnr, see below)
Edwin Spencer	250	
Henry Willis	50	
David Willis Jnr	50	
George Faber	156	
Alfred Faber	156	
Arthur Allan	125	
Hubert Faber	63	

Edwin Spencer's allocation was doubtless a reflection of his importance to the business. From the beginning the Directors described themselves as Life Directors, which signified share ownership. They were, however, colloquially known as 'the Partners' (this continued until the firm became publicly listed in 1976). David Willis became Chairman. The combined business was conducted from 32 Cornhill, where the complement of broking and underwriting staff numbered no more than a hundred people.

The Nineteenth Century

In September 1898, nine months after the merger which formed Willis, Faber, Edwin Spencer and Arthur Allan sailed to New York for another meeting with Johnson & Higgins. The proposal put forward by Johnson & Higgins was for a complete amalgamation. This was treated cautiously by the Board of Willis Faber, and in the event, not proceeded with. It was agreed, though, that Willis Faber and Johnson & Higgins should pool profits. To compensate Tyson's for their loss of the Johnson & Higgins business, it was agreed they would be paid between £1,250 and £1,500 per annum out of the joint profits for a period of five years.

Another of Edwin Spencer's great triumphs occurred in 1899 when he secured the appointment of Willis Faber to take over the agency of the Tokio Marine Insurance Company. He had assiduously cultivated Kenkichi Kagami, a young man sent to London by Tokio Marine to sort out the problems caused by his predecessor, who had appointed unsuitable agents. During his four years' stay in the City Kagami got to know Edwin Spencer and formed a great respect for his underwriting abilities. It was through Spencer that, in 1897, Tokio Marine appointed Johnson & Higgins as its agents in San Francisco. Kagami's career also flourished, and in 1922 he became Chairman of Tokio Marine.

The Willis relationship with Tokio Marine was to prove a major driving force in the twentieth century, and the prestige and importance of the Japanese account to Willis continues to this day.

———◈———

CHAPTER TWO

1900–1910

Willis Faber's net profit in 1900 was £48,454 on income of £70,710, an eye-watering margin of almost 70 per cent. As there was no taxation on company profits at that time, the profit was all distributed to the Directors. The first decade of the new century was an exciting one in the firm's development, with overseas expansion and the forming of Cornhill Insurance Company.

Arthur Allan took charge of the Marine Department, assisted by George Stamp on the brokerage side and by Herbert Worsley in charge of claims. Both Stamp and Worsley became Life Directors in 1903. The non-marine side of the business, known as the Fire Department, was run by Walter Faber. Edwin Spencer devoted himself almost exclusively to agency underwriting. The relationship with Johnson & Higgins was cemented and put on a more formal footing in December 1900 when there was another meeting in Southampton involving Stephen Loines and John D. Barratt, now President of Johnson & Higgins, and David Willis and Edwin Spencer of Willis Faber. The outcome of this meeting was the Exclusive Agreement, or Southampton Agreement, which formed the basis of the relationship between the two firms for the next ninety years.

In essence, Willis Faber was to refuse all American marine insurance business from any other source. As Johnson & Higgins had promised in April 1899 to use no English broker other than Willis Faber, exclusivity was established. Over the next three years attempts were made to enshrine the Agreement in a legal document, but this proved difficult. Finally, on 16 July 1903, David Willis wrote in frustration to James B. Dickson, the new President of Johnson & Higgins, proclaiming, 'To frame a legal document to the satisfaction of lawyers seems such an interminable business that personally I feel inclined to revert to your idea of having a more informal understanding that we divide our joint profits from every source in the proportions agreed upon.' He went on to point out that one advantage of an unwritten agreement was that either party could simply withdraw from the relationship if dissatisfied. One month later Dickson replied, 'We have long since been disgusted with the technicalities which the legal fraternity are so insistent upon including in documents of this character . . . It would seem to me as if an informal understanding would answer every purpose.' And that was that. Thereafter these two great firms worked together without ever signing a formal agreement.

Over the next few years there were a number of further meetings which clarified different issues. In 1924 Johnson & Higgins's President William Harvell La Boyteaux sought to put the principles onto a single sheet of paper for the first time. He drafted a memo which he called 'the idea of the agreement as it was intended'. The memo stated four simple points:

1 the arrangement was exclusive
2 either party was free to cancel it at any time
3 neither party was to depart from the agreement without consulting the other
4 neither party was to circumvent the agreement to secure new business or a new market.

There was also more vague speculation regarding a merger between the two firms, but this came to nothing. What is known is that, at some point, Johnson & Higgins suggested that Willis Faber should merge with the London broking firm of C. T. Bowring, who had become serious competitors. Edwin Spencer pursued this but it did not materialise.

Walter Faber regularly exhorted the Board to expand the company's non-marine interests. The upshot of this was that in May 1905 they registered Cornhill Insurance Company with a capital of £100,000. Its registered office was 31 Cornhill. The Directors and Shareholders were the same as those of Willis Faber, together with Walter Faber and Raymond Willis, who held 15 per cent and 10 per cent respectively. David Willis was Chairman and all Willis Faber Chairmen were to hold this post until 1947. The Cornhill prospered. In 1910 *Policy Holder* commented, 'The Cornhill has now completed the fourth year of its operations and we have much pleasure in stating that so far it has secured a profit ratio which is unusually high for an insurance company and particularly noticeable when compared with the results of other young offices.'

With his background and connections Arthur Allan naturally took a great interest in Canada and the opportunities it presented. In 1905 he obtained the important Canadian Pacific ocean fleet as a client. In June 1906 an office was opened in Montreal to service the Canadian Pacific account, and also to develop new business, both marine and non-marine.

The first radio equipment on a Canadian Pacific ship was installed on the *Empress of Britain* in 1906. Supplied by what was to become another Willis Faber client, the Marconi Wireless Telegraph Company, similar equipment was installed throughout the fleet; it enabled the dramatic arrest in July 1910 of the notorious murderer Dr Crippen and his mistress Ethel le Neve, following a wireless message from Canadian Pacific's steamer *Montrose* to Scotland Yard. The captain had recognised Crippen and also le Neve, even though she was dressed as a boy. It was the first time that wireless telegraphy had been used in the arrest of a criminal. Crippen was duly apprehended on his arrival in Canada.

By this time, Johnson & Higgins had substantial business in Canada. In order to avoid conflict between the two firms the Canadian Pool was established. This provided that all net profits arising from new business in Canada would be pooled and shared equally. The Canadian Pacific ocean fleet and Johnson & Higgins's average adjusting business were excluded from this arrangement.

Raymond Willis, appointed 'Chief Agent of the Company in the province of Quebec', greatly expanded the Canadian business, both marine and non-marine, and in August 1910 decided to replace the branch operation with a separate company, Willis Faber & Company of Canada Ltd. Its first Directors were Arthur Allan, Herbert Worsley, Raymond Willis, and Dale Harris of the Company's Montreal lawyers. On his return to England in 1911 Raymond Willis was appointed a Life Director.

Closer to home, in December 1907 the Willis Faber Board approved an agreement between Walter Schües of the Hamburg firm of Carstens & Schües to form Willis Faber & Schües to carry on business as marine and fire insurance brokers in that city. John Turvill moved to Hamburg to run the non-marine side of the business. Norddeutscher Lloyd of Bremen, one of the great trans-Atlantic liner companies, is thought to have been a client. What is known is that reinsurance business was handled by the Company. The venture turned out to be highly profitable.

The decade following the death of Queen Victoria in January 1901 saw the changing of the managerial guard. By the end of 1910 the three Faber brothers – George, Alfred and Walter – had retired, George to pursue a political career, while Walter became

Foreign Fire Manager of the Provincial Insurance Company as well as managing his own syndicate at Lloyd's. Subsequently Walter became Chairman of Lloyd's Non Marine Association between 1915 and 1919.

Edwin Spencer had indifferent health, and this forced his premature retirement in 1911 at the age of fifty-two. The Chairmanship of Willis would have been a fitting climax to his brilliant career, but it was not to be. He left the company a mere seventeen days before David Willis expressed his intention to retire. Arthur Allan (1867–1934) became Chairman in 1911, a position he held for twenty-three years till his death in 1934. Spencer remained a Director of Willis Faber, though not a shareholder, until 1921. During the 1914–18 Great War Spencer worked with W. E. Hargreaves of Bowrings in running the British Government's War Risks Scheme. His *Recollections*, addressed to his son, John Ogilvie Spencer, who had joined Willis Faber, were published in 1925. He died at Hove in June 1931 after a long and painful illness. John Spencer was not suited to a life in insurance and was asked to leave the firm in 1938. He was killed in Normandy in 1944 by a sniper whilst serving with the 2nd (Armoured) Battalion Welsh Guards. Julian Faber was a brother-officer.

CHAPTER THREE

✦•✦

1911–1928

By 1911 Willis Faber had a huge marine account, reputedly the largest broking portfolio in the world. They held, either direct or by way of reinsurance: the main American and Japanese fleets, via Johnson & Higgins and Tokio Marine respectively; the largest Canadian fleet, with Canadian Pacific; most of the British, German and Dutch liner companies serving the North Atlantic route – Cunard, White Star, Anchor, Allan, Norddeutscher Lloyd, Holland America – and other major shipping lines including Royal Mail and Union Castle. Missing from this glittering array were the great French companies, of which Dumas & Wylie had a virtual monopoly in the London market.

This was a golden period for the building of luxury liners. Cunard had built *Mauretania* and *Lusitania*, encouraged by the British Government who were concerned about the expansion of the German fleet. In order to compete, White Star Line commissioned Harland & Wolff of Belfast, another client of the firm, to build *Olympic* and *Titanic*, each of 46,000 tons. They were launched in Belfast in 1911 and 1912 respectively. Willis Faber placed the insurance for White Star Line, the hull and machinery sum insured being £1 million on each. RMS *Titanic* left Southampton on 10th April 1912 carrying 1,316 passengers and 885 crew. On the night of 14/15 April she struck the submerged spur of an iceberg four hundred miles east of the Grand Banks off Newfoundland. This great 'unsinkable' ship went down in two hours

RMS *Titanic*

and forty minutes with the loss of 1,490 lives. The Lloyd's Loss Book entry for 16th April reads: 'Titanic. British mail Southampton for New York foundered April 15 about 2-20 am in lat 41.16 North long 50.15 West after collision with ice. (Reported by wireless from Olympic to the Cape Race wireless station.) Further reports state that the loss of life is very serious.' Willis Faber arranged settlement of the claim within 30 days.

On 28 June 1914 Archduke Franz Ferdinand of Austro-Hungary was assassinated in the Bosnian capital of Sarajevo by Gavrilo Princip, a Serbian nationalist. Events developed rapidly, involving all the great powers of Europe. On 4 August Germany invaded neutral Belgium. Britain was bound by treaty obligations to defend Belgium, and declared war on Germany the same day. Of a total Willis Faber staff of 243, 125 joined His Majesty's forces. Thirty-eight were to die in action, including Raymond Willis, who was killed in Flanders in 1918. The number wounded and maimed is not known. Still, thirty-eight men killed represented 15 per cent of the total staff in 1914.

Apart from the inevitable loss of German business, there was a further loss of business as the British Government assumed 80 per cent of war risks on hulls and 100 per cent of the risks of requisitioned vessels, which included most of the great liners, used as troopships or hospital ships. Notwithstanding this, Willis Faber prospered during the Great War due to considerable expansion of cargo insurance. There was also profitable development in extending fire insurance policies to include damage by air raids. Net profit after taxation in 1918 was £124,291 on income of £522,848.

Arthur Allan and George Stamp, Deputy Chairman, dominated the firm in the period covered by this chapter. Their characters could not have been more different. Arthur Allan was by reputation kind, quietly spoken and courteous to all, whether junior clerk or important underwriter. Whilst maintaining an appropriate distance, he inspired great respect and devotion. George Stamp, by contrast, was by all accounts caustic and generally disliked. He was a strong character and, as will be shown, drove the expansion of the firm during his long tenure. He had become a Life Director in 1903 and, like Arthur Allan, was a protégé of Alfred Faber. It was George Stamp who instituted the 'Partners' Tea'. For over sixty years on each working day all Life Directors not absent from London were required to take tea together at 4.15 p.m. prompt. His determination is shown by the story that when told by his local golf club that there was a waiting list for membership, he promptly bought it. He took personal

Arthur Allan

charge of recruiting talent to the firm. It was he who deter-
minedly pursued and acquired the services of Felix Weisz in 1925.
The latter's contribution to the success of Willis Faber will be told
in detail later.

There was an enormous disparity of rewards within the firm.
In 1921 Arthur Allan was paid £49,375. In addition he would
have received substantial dividends as a Director of both Willis
Faber and Cornhill. The top salary earned at that time by an
Ordinary Director (one level below Life Director and without a
shareholding) was Fred Bartlett's: he was paid £2000, plus a
profit-sharing bonus of around 18 per cent. By contrast, the
salary scale for clerks ranged from £100 a year at the age of

32

twenty to £250 a year at the age of thirty-five. A discretionary bonus, paid at Christmas and in the spring, ranged between 10 and 15 per cent. Doubtless these enormous pay differentials narrowed with the passage of time. There is, though, a story from the 1960s of a junior broker in the Aviation Division, who was later to rise to eminence in the firm, declining a salary increase on the grounds that he did not wish to infringe his amateur status.

Willis Faber expanded in 1922 with the formation of Willis Faber & Partners. This was the brainchild of George Stamp and Kenkichi Kagami and was devised to enable Willis to arrange reciprocal fire reinsurance treaties with British and Continental companies for Tokio Marine and its affiliated companies. The first of these treaties was arranged with Generali of Trieste. Other clients followed, notably Norwich Union and Liverpool, London & Globe. The timing of these reinsurance treaties proved to be fortunate. The Great Kanto earthquake, which occurred on 2 September 1923, killed 150,000 people and destroyed Yokohama and most of Tokyo. The underlying financial strength of Tokio Marine, supported by its reinsurance treaties, enabled it to survive and prosper.

Many of Willis Faber's clients were based or had their home port in Liverpool. These included Cunard, White Star, Royal Mail, Brocklebank and Ocean Steam Ship. The company had for many years done business with Brodrick Leitch & Kendall, marine insurance brokers in Liverpool which had been formed by the merger of three broker firms in 1876. Willis wished to have a presence in Liverpool, so a minority shareholding was acquired in 1921; this was converted to a majority holding in 1933 and full ownership in 1969.

Henry L. Riseley & Sons was one of the first broking houses in the West Country. It had been founded in Bristol in 1868 by Henry Lorymer Riseley, who had started his insurance career with Norwich Union aged thirteen. The firm expanded by opening offices in Cardiff and Birmingham. George Stamp decided that Willis Faber's non-marine business needed more development, and in 1921 he recruited Fred Bartlett, then Riseley's Resident Partner in Cardiff. This upset Riseley's and they complained to George Stamp. He assured them that Bartlett would not seek direct business in the West Country, Wales and the Midlands. This was not really satisfactory for either Willis Faber or Riseley's. The upshot was that in November 1922 Willis Faber acquired the business and Frank and Arthur Riseley were appointed Life Directors. The offices in Bristol, Cardiff and Birmingham continued to operate under the Riseley name for another half-century. The three Riseley brothers were outstanding tennis players. Frank was runner-up in the Wimbledon singles championship in 1903, 1904 and 1906 and won the doubles with Sydney Smith in 1906. Arthur Riseley was chairman of the All England Lawn Tennis & Croquet Club 1953–5.

In January 1923 the whole of the marine and non-marine brokerage staff moved to the first floor of a splendid new building, 54 Leadenhall Street. Over the years Willis Faber progressively took on further floors. It was the Head Office of Willis until the move to Ten Trinity Square in 1977.

There was a major test of the relationship with Johnson & Higgins in 1928 when they acquired Balfour, Guthrie & Co., a San Francisco-based marine broker. Balfour Guthrie had a long-standing relationship in London with Sedgwick and wished to continue placing business with them. It took the personal intervention of the President of Johnson & Higgins, William Harvell La Boyteaux, to persuade them otherwise. In the gentlemanly spirit of the times, Willis paid Sedgwick the brokerage to which they felt entitled.

CHAPTER FOUR

———◈———

1929–1945

On 1 January 1929 Willis Faber & Company merged with Dumas & Wylie Limited. The history of Dumas & Wylie really began when Henri Dumas left Barings in 1824 and set up in business at the Baltic Coffee House in Threadneedle Street as a merchant trading in commodities with Hamburg. Business clearly prospered; a few years later he married and bought a house in fashionable rural Clapham. From the beginning he placed cargo insurance business at Lloyd's through his brother-in-law Alexander Wylie, whose office was at 34 Lombard Street. Henri Dumas died aged forty-nine in May 1843. He was buried in the vaults below Holy Trinity, the Parish Church of Clapham, of which he was a benefactor. His widow, Eliza, founded the Lloyd's broking firm of Dumas & Wylie, taking James Leverton Wylie into Partnership. Wylie became a prominent figure at Lloyd's and served on the Committee for twenty-five years.

Henry John Phillip Dumas (Henry II) joined the firm in 1847 aged eighteen and became a Partner six years later. His oldest son, Henry John Fairrie Dumas (Henry III), joined in 1879 and became a Partner after eight years. In 1881 Dumas & Wylie merged with Augustus de Chapeaurouge & Co., and one year later Augustus became a Partner. His father, Philippe Augustus de Chapeaurouge, was a fellow Huguenot and friend of Henri Dumas. They became related by marriage when Philippe married Henri's sister-in-law. Dumas & Wylie Limited, as they became in

35

1900, had built a great marine business. France was their principal source of business, and they had a virtual monopoly of the largest French fleets. Important business was also conducted in Norway, Sweden and the Netherlands.

There was a feeling in Dumas & Wylie that they needed to join someone larger, as they were concerned about their exposure to unpaid premiums. In 1928 Raymond Dumas initiated merger discussions with Willis Faber. Arthur Allan and George Stamp were attracted both to the outstanding portfolio of business and to the opportunity to acquire a person with the talents of Raymond Dumas. Agreement was reached within ten days. Four members of the Dumas family – Henry John Fairrie, Gerald, Raymond and Basil – joined the Board of Willis Faber & Co. and subsequently became Life Directors of the merged company, Willis Faber & Dumas Limited. The seventy-five staff of Dumas & Wylie moved from 78 Gracechurch Street and joined their new colleagues at 54 Leadenhall Street. In the first year of the merged company, net profit after tax was £207,453, on income of £470,692.

Arthur Allan died suddenly in March 1934 of pneumonia. He was greatly liked, respected and admired, not just within the firm but also by clients and the market. An obituary notice read, 'It was not only as a broker that Mr Allan was a great Lloyd's man, for he was also a tremendous influence for good in the market. He stood for absolute integrity and impartiality, and in addition he had a charm of manners and a kindliness of nature that made him friends wherever he went.' George Stamp (1868–1939) succeeded him as Chairman.

Willis Faber's pre-eminent position in marine insurance was further reinforced by the merger with Dumas & Wylie. Prestige was then added through arranging the insurance of the two great Cunard liners: *Queen Mary*, launched in 1934, and *Queen*

George Stamp

Elizabeth, in 1938. The Directors of Willis Faber & Dumas were invited to both launches.

George Stamp was determined, though, to expand the firm's non-marine business, and his relentless pursuit of Felix Weisz epitomised this. Weisz was born in Vienna in 1889 at the height of the Austro-Hungarian Empire. He was described as gifted with an extraordinary intelligence, firmness of purpose and great integrity. In the mid-1920s he was working in Istanbul and employed by a British firm called Back & Manson, agents in Turkey for the Assicurazioni Generali of Trieste. So keen were Willis to obtain his services that in November 1925 they acquired Back & Manson, and so Felix came to London. Two years after his arrival in England he changed his name to Lex Douglas-Whyte, combining part of his Scottish wife's maiden name with an anglicised version of his own. He had no contract or letter of appointment

37

and no idea of what he was to be paid. When he raised this with George Stamp, then Deputy Chairman, he was told he would be paid 20 per cent more than he had been at Back & Manson, without Stamp enquiring what that figure was, and to sort it out with the Chief Accountant.

He was appointed Manager of a new Foreign Fire Department, and spent the next thirty years with the firm. Some years later he received a handwritten letter from Arthur Allan dated 18 December 1933:

My dear Douglas-Whyte,

I have been asked by the other Directors to tell you that – subject to your acceptance – you have been elected to be a Director of Willis Faber & Dumas Ltd as from 1st January next.

We all hope that this proposal is one that will be as agreeable to you as it is to us to make it; and that we may congratulate ourselves on the acquisition of a colleague in whom we all have the most complete confidence.

You will naturally want to have some idea of how you will be affected materially by becoming a Director, so I may explain that it is proposed to allocate you:

8000 shares at 33 shillings each	£13,200
1500 shares at 10 shillings each	£750
365 redeemable preference at £1 each	£365
	£14,315

Unless there is a rather violent deterioration in the business these shares should yield £7,000 per annum in round figures, subject to income and surtax.

The payment for the shares could be spread over the next few years as may be convenient to you out of yearly profits, interest being debited to you on the amount unpaid at the rate of 5 per cent per annum.

So as to make the payment a little easier we are proposing to allot to you 1500 of the unissued shares of the company at 10 shillings per share and I think I should explain that from the moment these shares are made over to you, they become automatically of the value of 33 shillings per share and will remain of this value unless for some good reason the Directors decide to vary the value at which the shares of retiring or deceased Directors are to be taken over by the remaining Directors.

The question of the value of the shares for this purpose is decided at a Board Meeting held annually in July.

Remaining yours

A. C. Allan

There are two noteworthy features about this letter. First, the fact that it is handwritten by the Chairman, and second, that it reveals an extraordinary expected annual return of almost 50 per cent on the shareholding.

Lex Douglas-Whyte was the architect of the great non-marine reinsurance business that Willis has to this day, forging relationships in Europe, North and South America, and Japan. To quote Digby Brindle-Wood-Williams, 'His very name opened every door and insurance companies were proud if they could entrust their reinsurance needs to him.' He was also the mentor of Edward Gumbel, who will appear later in this book.

Frederick Passmore was Company Secretary and Chief Accountant. He was reputedly a hard taskmaster, and a summons to his office was not something the clerks relished. He was also a man of few words, as this letter to a slow-paying client attests:

Dear Sir,

Remit.

Yours faithfully

F. G. Passmore

The *Hindenburg* burns in New Jersey, May 1937

Fred Bartlett ran the Direct Department, which managed commercial and industrial clients. He and his assistant, Henry Tunstill, travelled the United Kingdom energetically developing fire business, particularly from heavy industries. They were helped in this by the work of Frank Dyall, who formed the Survey Department, which was seen as a considerable innovation. Frank Dyall was the brother of the well-known actor Valentine Dyall, famous for his radio role as 'The Man in Black'. Henry Tunstill had joined the firm in 1917 as a policy typist. (It was not until

40

years later that women were employed for this kind of work. Even then a woman was not allowed to work in the firm if her husband was already employed there.) The Accident Department, which today would be described as the Casualty Department, had a strong focus on workers' compensation. It also looked after the fledgling aviation business. In May 1937 the great German airship *Hindenburg* was destroyed and Willis collected the claim as reinsurance of their client, Deutsche Luftpool.

Douglas Langmead joined the firm in 1920, eventually retiring aged seventy-eight. He had a wide business development role with a special commission-sharing arrangement. He was instrumental, with Fred Bartlett, in the formation of the Life and Pensions Department, which became the responsibility of Dick Denby. This grew into an increasingly important business, and Dick Denby was made a Life Director in 1948. A further development in the non-marine area came with motor insurance. The introduction of the Road Traffic Act 1930, which instituted compulsory motor insurance, resulted in a great expansion of business.

George Stamp's long career came to end with his retirement in December 1937. He was succeeded by Henry Willis (1876–1947), the son of David Willis, first Chairman of Willis, Faber & Company Limited. Henry Willis had spent the greater part of his career managing the marine underwriting side of the business.

The 1930s were marked as the decade of global economic depression and the growing threat of war in Europe. The leadership of the firm may have been autocratic but there was a strong paternalistic streak as well. Despite mass unemployment there was a policy of no layoffs. Interestingly, Johnson & Higgins had a similar policy.

On 1 September 1939 Germany invaded Poland. Two days later Britain and France declared war; George Stamp died that same day. Around three hundred staff joined the armed forces.

Henry Willis

The majority of those left behind were evacuated; Marine to the Golf Club at Stoke Poges and Non-Marine to the Hotel de Paris in Bray-on-Thames. A skeleton staff remained at Leadenhall Street to carry on broking, as well as air-raid fire-watching. Just as had happened in the First World War, large amounts of business were lost, notably from Generali, Jauch & Hübener, Tokio Marine and Taisho Marine. This was, to some extent, replaced by focusing on the United States and the United Kingdom. Lloyd's remained a war risks market, where, predictably, rates soared. Raymond Willis, ever the master marine broker, had placed, within hours of the occupation of Norway, a facility enabling all Norwegian merchant vessels not seized by the Germans to be fully covered. It was said that when Raymond Willis entered Lloyd's to broke the Cunard fleet the underwriters would rise to their feet. This reflected both his personal standing and the prestige of Willis Faber & Dumas.

CHAPTER FIVE

—➤·◦·◄—

1946–1975

After the war ended, the offices in Stoke Poges and Bray-on-Thames were closed and the staff transferred back to London. Staff who been in the Armed Forces gradually returned, although demobilisation was, for many a frustratingly slow process. Fourteen men did not return; their names are recorded on the war memorial which is now in the Auditorium of the Willis Building in Lime Street. The memorial also records the names of those staff from both Willis Faber and Dumas & Wylie who were killed in the Great War.

Lex Douglas-Whyte and Edward Gumbel, master and devoted pupil, had planned for this time, and together they spent the next few years rebuilding global relationships as well as forging new ones. Both sat on the market committee that formulated the legal framework to deal with the complex and arduous process of settling pre-war liabilities for unpaid premiums and unsettled claims. Inevitably many records had been lost. Douglas-Whyte believed that the London market had to be seen to honour its obligations, and Willis Faber paid the market many of the client debts themselves. This remarkably generous act was also commercially astute since it served to add to the firm's prestige and reputation.

H. Eduard Gumbel, who was always known as Edward, was born in Bingen-on-the-Rhine. His father was manager of the Disconto-Gesellschaft Bank. Edward had a glittering academic career. He attended universities in Geneva, Berlin, Heidelberg, Zurich and the London School of Economics. In 1935 he graduated *magna cum laude* from Zurich University as its youngest-ever Doctor of Laws. He came back to England in 1936 to read for the Bar and was admitted to the Middle Temple as a student in 1937. He was carrying with him a letter of introduction to Lex Douglas-Whyte. As a result he joined Willis Faber & Dumas Limited in November of the same year, being attached to Mr Holland's Non-Marine Claims Department. After six months he was told by Lex Douglas-Whyte, 'Mr Holland informs me that you are being useful. We ought to pay you now rather than in another six months' time. How much do you need to live on?' The response was £3 a week, which Douglas-Whyte found reasonable, but the next day he came back crestfallen and told Gumbel, 'The Chairman does not think we can pay you more than £120.'

Gumbel's father had lost his job after the Nazi party came to power in 1933. As the persecution of Jews became increasingly harsh, Edward finally persuaded his parents to leave Germany, and they arrived in England in March 1939 with the few belongings that they were allowed to take with them. It was a close-run thing: had they stayed they would almost certainly have been victims of the Holocaust. Because he had not completed his naturalisation, Edward Gumbel was interned in May 1940 as a holder of a passport from an enemy country. Willis lobbied hard for his release, which took place in October of that year. They also paid his salary to his parents in this six-month period. Gumbel used the time on the Isle of Man where he had been interned to good effect, studying for the Bar finals and adding Spanish to the three languages he already spoke. In spring 1941 he was awarded the certificate of honour in the final Bar examination. In 1946 he and his wife Ellen became British citizens and in 1947 he was called to the Bar.

In his book *Recollections of My Personal Life*, Edward Gumbel describes the task he and Lex Douglas-Whyte had set themselves as follows:

To reconstruct WF&D's portfolio in Germany and the rest of Europe; to repair the bridges that had traditionally connected the firm with these countries and most importantly, also, Japan; to reinforce the new connections DW had started in South and North America; to maintain and expand WF&D's role in the global network whereby reinsurance acted as the universal distributor of risks – such were the tasks we saw ahead for us, for the London market; for the companies in many countries who were or might become our clients.

The size, strength and reputation of the reinsurance business today is testament to their achievements.

The wartime evacuation to Bray-on-Thames and Stoke Poges had been managed by Guy Wilson. He was with Urwick Orr & Partners, one of the pioneers of management consulting, who in 1937 were engaged to reorganise the office. He remained with Willis Faber and introduced the Hollerith mechanised accounting system, which remained in use until 1969. Universally known as GBW, he became Company Secretary and effectively ran the administrative side of the firm. What is now called Human Resources was then known as the Staff Department and this also came under GBW. Martyn Hedley left Eton in 1961 and, after a year contract gardening, joined the firm in 1962. On his first day he was told by GBW, 'Aviation, Hedley. I will try and get you into a gentleman's department as soon as possible.' The gentleman's department was, of course, Marine. Apart from a brief spell in underwriting, Martyn spent his career in what is now Aerospace, leading it to its present global eminence. No important management decision was made by the Chairman without consulting

45

Guy Wilson, Donald Cann (of the auditors Baker Sutton) and Dick Millett (of the law firm Millett and Company), a reflection of the esteem and trust in which they were held.

The experience of the move to Bray-on-Thames and Stoke Poges encouraged Willis to open an out-of-town office at Leigh-on-Sea in 1947. In subsequent expansion, offices were opened at Westcliff and then Southend. By 1970 there were around 600 staff in Southend, engaged principally in back office functions such as accounting and policy production.

Henry Willis died in July 1947 and was succeeded by Raymond Dumas (1886–1971), who had joined Dumas & Wylie in 1906. Educated at Winchester, Raymond Dumas joined the family firm immediately upon leaving school. His entire career was spent with Dumas & Wylie which subsequently became Willis Faber & Dumas. This was interrupted by service in the Great War, with the 60th Division. He went to France in 1916, thence briefly to Salonika and then to Palestine, where he fought in General Allenby's campaign against the Turks.

Whilst the post-war years saw a rapid rebuilding of the world's merchant fleet, the 1950s and 1960s saw the gradual reduction of the dominance of marine insurance in the firm. Reinsurance grew in importance, and this was accentuated by countries which had previously sent insurance business direct to London now developing their own markets. At the same time, aviation grew in importance with the introduction of the jet airliner and the era of mass travel. The post-war era also saw the expansion of the UK branch network, both by acquisition and by the opening of new offices. These included Warrington, Cheltenham, Glasgow, Sheffield, Newcastle, Dublin, Belfast and Manchester.

There was further expansion in underwriting. This included the acquisition of several Lloyd's syndicates, notably Towers and Whittall. Sir Henry Mance (later Chairman of Lloyd's, 1969–72)

Raymond Dumas on a visit to Japan

came to Willis through this acquisition. Allianz International became an underwriting client in 1974. All underwriting activities became grouped under Willis Faber Underwriting Management, which encompassed Sovereign Marine & General, and owned Lloyd's syndicates and the insurance companies for whom Willis acted as underwriting agents. Mance was also to be Chairman of this new grouping.

Abroad, Willis Faber entered South Africa in 1951, Australia in 1958 and New Zealand in 1969. Retail expansion in other

Mr and Mrs Raymond Dumas and Elwyn Rhys on a visit to Canada

parts of the world was not pursued for fear of disturbing reinsurance relationships. The implications of this, particularly with regard to the relationship with Johnson & Higgins, are examined later.

Raymond Dumas retired at the end of 1954. Lionel Broad, Marine Life Director, paid this tribute: 'As a marine broker he was head and shoulders above his rivals and within his own company he was considered supreme.' He was, though, a complex character, and both Lex Douglas-Whyte and Edward Gumbel's relationships with him were difficult.

He was succeeded as Chairman by Elwyn Rhys (1900–66), another Marine Life Director, who had joined the Non-Marine

48

Elwyn Rhys

Department in the 1920s. Rhys was educated at Eton and, before joining the firm, spent time in Hamburg, becoming fluent in German. He was the younger son of Baron Dynevor, and his family were of ancient lineage: Sir Rhys ap Thomas fought with Henry Tudor at the Battle of Bosworth Field in 1485. Elwyn Rhys enlisted in the army in 1939 and served with the Welsh Guards, rising to the rank of Major. At the end of the war he returned to insurance broking. There is little on record about his Chairmanship, although Edward Gumbel described him as great gentleman, perceptive, thoughtful and scrupulously fair. John Prentice, a Marine Life Director who rose to become Deputy Chairman, noted, 'I always had the feeling that Willis Faber to him was

Derek Ripley

something that happened when one was not shooting.' When Dorrance Sexton made his first visit to London as Chairman of Johnson & Higgins, Elwyn Rhys was, indeed, shooting in Wales. He had apparently forgotten to tell his colleagues about the visit and Lionel Broad was left with the job of looking after Sexton.

Elwyn Rhys retired at the end of 1965 and died within a month. Horace Derek de Chapeaurouge Ripley, commonly known as Derek Ripley (1910–67), became Chairman in 1966 after having been a Marine Life Director. He was educated at Harrow and joined Dumas & Wylie shortly before the merger with Willis Faber. He was a descendant of Augustus Charles de Chapeaurouge, who had in 1881 merged his broking business with Dumas & Wylie. Derek Ripley spoke excellent French. He was first and foremost a top-class broker and had the reputation of being able, reserved and kind. His first task as Chairman was to restore relations with Johnson & Higgins, which at the time were not very good. He and Dorrance Sexton rapidly became great friends. They sorted out any number of unresolved and contentious issues, and forbade bickering between each other's subordinates. The separate operations in Canada were merged. But in September 1967 Derek Ripley died suddenly of a heart attack in the South of France where he was on holiday. This was a great tragedy and altered the course of Willis Faber's history. Had he lived he might have achieved, as John Prentice expressed it, 'the dreamed-of union with Johnson & Higgins. Derek and Dorrance might well have pulled it off where lesser men have failed.'

John Roscoe succeeded Derek Ripley and had the distinction of being the first Chairman not from the Marine Department. Edward Gumbel described the process thus: 'The choice of the WF&D Chairman was a time-honoured and gentlemanly ritual. Nothing as vulgar as a vote would see the light of day. Instead he emerged from a diplomatic sounding of Board opinion by one of the senior members who did not himself have presidential ambitions.'

Overseas travel was another gentlemanly ritual. Limited to a privileged few, it was invariably in first class and, until the 1960s, by ship, with all the associated comforts. Towards the end of a colourful career, a Deputy Chairman recalled asking for instructions before embarking on his first overseas trip as a young marine broker. In summary these were to eat and drink what was put in front of him, to entertain the ladies and not to come back with a sun tan. Apparently these were the only instructions he ever received.

John Roscoe

John Townsend Roscoe (1913–84) was educated at Marl-
borough and Trinity College, Oxford. He saw war service with the
8th Army in North Africa and became a Major in the Queen's
Royal (West Surrey) Regiment. After the war he returned to
insurance broking. In 1951 he was broking aviation business at
Stewart Smith when he was recruited by Lex Douglas-Whyte to
join Willis and head the Aviation Department. John Roscoe laid
the foundations of what is today the firm's prestigious global
Aerospace business, and it was he who carved out the world market for the enormous values needed for the Boeing 747 jumbo jets.

Many years before John Roscoe became Chairman there were
concerns about the firm's ability to maintain its private status. As

The Willis Faber and Dumas Board, 1970; *standing, L–R*: Ted Hann (Baker Sutton & Co.), David Palmer, Dick Bowes, John Prentice; *seated, L–R*: Edward Gumbel, Henry Dumas, John Roscoe, Julian Faber, Ronnie Taylor

explained earlier, for most of its long history the Life Directors owned all the shares in the firm. They purchased shares when they became Life Directors and upon retirement sold them to existing or new Life Directors. There were few of these, and at one point Raymond Dumas owned 30 per cent of the shares. They saw themselves as stewards with the responsibility of passing the firm on to the next generation in better shape than they had found it.

To improve liquidity and also to enable Life Directors to

capitalise on their shareholdings, in 1963 25 per cent of the equity share capital was sold to a number of leading financial institutions; this was increased to 40 per cent in 1971. The established practice of share sales between Life Directors was severely tested when, within less than three years, Elwyn Rhys retired and Dick Denby and Derek Ripley died. In 1965, David Palmer, Ronnie Taylor and John Prentice purchased the dying Dick Denby's 12 per cent shareholding, each paying £6,000 for a 4 per cent share. The Board decided it was necessary to broaden the shareholder base, and on 1 January 1972 fifteen new Life Directors were appointed, drawn from across the firm. They purchased shares, some with the help of loans, from a pool provided by the existing Life Directors. At the same time, Kenneth Childs and Chris Hughes joined the Board.

Unlike his predecessors, John Roscoe did not travel extensively, mainly because he refused to fly – it is believed, because of a near-fatal wartime experience. New York and Moscow were pretty much the limits of his travels. When travelling by train in Europe he would take with him bottles of Malvern water and a special kettle so that he could make his own tea. He had a self-deprecating wit. As an accomplished French speaker, he would say, 'Moi, je parle tres bien français, mais je ne comprends pas un mot.' (I speak very good French but I do not understand a word.) He retired as Chairman at the end of 1971. This was earlier than expected and was brought about by a personal tragedy when people close to him were killed in a horrific motorway crash. He subsequently became Chairman of a Lloyd's Underwriting Agency. At his memorial service, John Prentice said of him, 'He was a brilliant broker, with a skill that is given to few, and a most consummate advocate. He would tolerate nothing which would in any way diminish the honour of the firm which he felt it was a high honour to serve.'

Julian Faber

Julian Tufnell Faber (1917–2002) succeeded John Roscoe as Chairman in 1972. He was the son of Alfred Faber, who had been a Partner of Faber Brothers and one of the original Directors of Willis Faber & Co. Limited. Both Arthur Allan and George Stamp were his godparents. Educated at Winchester and Trinity College, Oxford, he was an outstanding games player, excelling at cricket in the Winchester XI, and in the school rackets and golf teams. In 1935 he partnered A. B. Kingsley to win the Public Schools Rackets Championship at Queen's Club. He joined Willis Faber in 1938. During the Second World War he served in the Welsh Guards, seeing action in North-West Europe with the Guards Armoured Division, and rising to the rank of Major.

The six years of his Chairmanship were marked by significantly increased profits, the move to new offices in London and Ipswich and, most notably, the change from being a privately owned company to having the shares listed on the London Stock Exchange.

Lex Douglas-Whyte did not live to see these great changes. He had retired to Kelso in the Scottish Borders in 1956, perhaps disappointed that his brilliant career had not been crowned with the Chairmanship. He became active in local affairs and for a time served on Kelso Town Council. He died in May 1973, leaving his prized model railway to a local primary school. Edward Gumbel wrote of his great mentor, 'The debt which the firm owes to Lex Douglas-Whyte is considerable. With the support of John Turvill, who for many years was the Senior Partner of the non-marine side, he established the firm's position in the forefront of non-marine and aviation reinsurance and became the principal architect of its worldwide reputation.' He also said of working for him, 'His loyalty to his staff was unbounded and he measured us by standards almost as high as he applied to himself.'

C. T. Bowring & Company had long been respected and powerful competitors of Willis. They traced their history back to Benjamin Bowring, who set up as a watchmaker and jeweller in Exeter in 1811. An ambitious man, he went to the British colony of Newfoundland and established a shop there. Business expanded into importing goods such as stationery, soap and clothing, and later into the cod and seal oil trade. Ship-owning and insurance followed these activities. In 1971 Bowring acquired Bowmaker, a finance house specialising in consumer credit. The timing proved unfortunate. Two years later the secondary banking crisis erupted as interest rates rose sharply to combat rapidly-rising inflation. The secondary banks, particularly those which had lent heavily to fuel a commercial property boom, had to be rescued by the Bank of England in what was termed 'the lifeboat'. Bowmaker were put

Richard Purnell, Bill Nickolls and David Palmer on the formation
of WFJ&H Australia in 1970

in 'the lifeboat' with support of £89 million. Around this time
Willis progressively acquired, with the help of Morgan Grenfell,
a shareholding in Bowrings as the prelude to a possible bid. In
the event this was not proceeded with. There was the feeling that
it would not be fair to strike whilst Bowrings were vulnerable.
Transatlantic relationships, Bowrings with Marsh & McLennan
and Willis with Johnson & Higgins, were also seen as a major
impediment. One can only speculate how the broking landscape
would be today had Willis and Bowring merged to form a domi-
nant UK broking firm. As it was, after a protracted, and at times
acrimonious, struggle, Bowrings was acquired by Marsh in 1980.

The Willis Building in Ipswich

By 1970 Willis had 1,600 Staff in London and 650 in South-end. The long leases on Leadenhall Street would expire over the next decade. A decision was made to have a greater presence outside London, and the choice came down to expanding the existing offices in Southend or finding a new location. Southend was thought to be far too close to London. Moreover, there were potential planning difficulties as there were plans to locate a major international airport nearby. The choice narrowed down to Ipswich and Hastings; the Board voted for Ipswich. John Waite, the Company Secretary, and a group of trusted advisers set about

Harold Macmillan opening the Willis Building

acquiring the site, which had a number of owners.

The building at Ipswich was commissioned during the Chairmanship of John Roscoe and opened during that of Julian Faber. John Waite wrote to the Royal Institute of British Architects which provided him with a list of twelve architectural practices. John Roscoe and Julian Faber visited Norman Foster at Millwall Docks to view his project, the Fred Olsen Amenity Centre. Norman Foster & Partners were duly commissioned, and Foster credits John Roscoe as being pivotal to this. It was regarded as a remarkably bold move by what was generally considered a conservative group of men. The building, with its signature glass curtain wall and vast open plan, was a pioneering example of energy-conscious design that challenged the accepted thinking about office buildings. It was opened on 2 June 1975 by the former Prime Minister, and father-in-law of Julian Faber, Harold Macmillan. Around 450 jobs were transferred from Southend, which closed, and from London. Generous relocation packages were provided. Nine hundred people were recruited and trained locally over a period of two or three years. In a demonstration of Willis's commitment to the Ipswich project, Ronnie Taylor, Deputy Chairman, moved his home to nearby Tendring in Essex.

Norman Foster went on to achieve international acclaim with iconic buildings such as the Hong Kong & Shanghai Bank in Hong Kong, the Reichstag in Berlin and, in the United Kingdom, the Sainsbury Centre in Norwich, Stansted Airport and the Swiss Re building in St Mary Axe, universally known as 'The Gherkin'. Born in 1935 in Manchester, Foster came from a modest working-class family. He is now Baron Foster of Thames Bank, OM. The Willis Building, which laid the foundations of his reputation, was awarded Grade I Listed status in 1991, the youngest building ever to have won this accolade.

CHAPTER SIX

1976–1981

The year 1976 was a remarkable one in the history of the firm: a new London headquarters was purchased and the company's shares became publicly traded. In June contracts were completed for the purchase of the Port of London Authority building in Trinity Square, close by the Tower of London, designed by Sir Edwin Cooper to the commission of the PLA. It has variously been described as a 'wedding cake', 'one of London's most important buildings' and 'the nearest thing London has to the Vittore Emanuele monument in Rome'. Conceived as a perfect square, with the angle cut off towards Trinity Square, it displays craftsmanship redolent of a former age. The foundation stone was laid in 1915. The First World War delayed its completion, and it was formally opened by the Prime Minister, David Lloyd George, on 17 October 1922. During the Second World War it was occupied by the Royal Navy and suffered substantial damage from an air raid. In 1946 the Tower Room was used to host a reception to mark the first meeting of members of the United Nations.

The building was the headquarters of the PLA until 1970 when they moved down-river to Tilbury. It was purchased by Amalgamated Investment & Property Co. which modernised it to provide 170,000 square feet of space and renamed the building, somewhat unimaginatively, Amalgamated House. Amalgamated Investment also became victims of the secondary banking crisis. Their creditors sold the freehold building to Willis for £13.75

Ten Trinity Square

million, a knock-down price which sent shivers through the property market. It was renamed Ten Trinity Square.

In 1967 Willis and Morgan Grenfell exchanged shareholdings, with Willis taking a 10 per cent share in Morgan Grenfell, a prestigious merchant bank. Historically, Morgan Guaranty of New York was the only institutional shareholder, with Morgan Grenfell Directors past and present and their families holding the remainder. This was broadened in 1961 to include four institutional shareholders. The Willis 10 per cent was increased to 24 per cent in 1974 with the placing of the Morgan Guaranty shareholding.

Pre-tax profits increased from £2.2 million in 1967 to £7.7 million in 1974. In 1975, the last year as a private company, pre-tax profits were £10.2 million, derived as follows:

Insurance broking	£8.1 million
Underwriting	£1.1 million
Morgan Grenfell Dividends	£1.0 million

In August 1976 Willis announced that they planned to float their shares on the Stock Exchange. Johnson & Higgins were neither consulted nor informed in advance. They were not best pleased and their Chairman, Dick Purnell, accused Willis of selling their account. The offer document stated that no one client represented more than 10 per cent of the business, which came as a considerable surprise to Johnson & Higgins as they had always assumed that they represented at least 50 per cent.

The move towards becoming a public company is generally thought to have started during John Roscoe's chairmanship. The professional advisers quickly made plain that the accounting systems, management reporting and financial controls were simply not up to the standards required of a public company. Michael Julien was recruited from British Leyland, where he had been

Treasurer, to address these shortcomings. With remarkable energy he gathered together a team which completed the task in a little over two years, making possible the issue of the listing prospectus. The shares became publicly traded on 9 November 1976, opening at a price of 190p. The flotation created a number of millionaires, which was highlighted in the press. Johnson & Higgins's displeasure did not last long, as they acquired a 5 per cent shareholding.

The firm had long eschewed the glare of publicity, and whilst the name of Willis Faber & Dumas had been known to all insurance professionals, it had often been misquoted by clients. The author was once shown into the office of a client and introduced as 'Mr Claydon of Freeman Hardy & Willis', the shoe store chain whose shops were then on every high street. Once a public company, publicity became an inevitable accompaniment for the firm, now styled Willis Faber Limited.

This was also a successful year for the business, with pre-tax profits increasing 60 per cent from £10.15 million to £16.32 million and every area of activity proving to be buoyant. Sovereign Marine & General reversed its previous profit decline, and Lloyd's and Company agency business produced substantially greater profits, as did the associate companies in Australia, Canada and South Africa. The UK economic conditions helped flatter the performance. The decline in the value of sterling against other major currencies increased profits disproportionately, inflation raised insured values and very high interest rates produced strong investment income.

Pre-tax profits increased to £19.56 million in 1977. The Annual Report did, though, contain a warning that the costs associated with the Ipswich project and the acquisition of Ten Trinity Square were having a significant drag on profits. There was also mention of heavy expenditure to come from improving informa-

Ronnie Taylor (left) with the Grenadier Guards in Italy, 1944

tion technology. During 1977 associated companies in France, Iran and Dubai were established. A subsidiary was opened in Hong Kong, as was a representative office in Saudi Arabia, and a 49 per cent interest was acquired in Lloyd Armstrong & Ramsey, a Dublin-based insurance broker.

Julian Faber retired at the end of 1977 after a long and distinguished career. During his tenure the firm relinquished its 150-year-long private status and transformational decisions were made on properties. Edward Gumbel said of him, 'Intelligence, good judgement and great style imbued his years.' He was succeeded by Ronnie Taylor, who had been Deputy Chairman. David

Palmer was appointed Chief Executive; it was the first time the roles had been split.

Arthur Ronald Taylor (1921–2011) had what has rightly been described as a remarkable life. He was born in Wales, on the Marches west of Shrewsbury. Sent away to boarding school at the age of six-and-a-half, he then went on to Winchester. After one year at Trinity College, Oxford, he was accepted into the Royal Military Academy, Sandhurst, where he was awarded the Sword of Honour as best cadet. He was an outstanding games player, excelling at rackets, and a fine shot. Commissioned into the Grenadier Guards, he embarked for Tunisia with the 5th Battalion in March 1943 and saw action in North Africa. The Battalion then fought at Anzio, and in the long and bloody campaign up through Northern Italy that followed. After the war he saw service in Palestine and also attended Staff College. He left the army in 1953 through ill health, having twice been mentioned in dispatches and been awarded a military MBE. He managed to get a job with the broking firm of Lawrence Phillips. Quickly mastering life and pensions business, he was approached to join Willis Faber & Dumas, which he did in 1959. His responsibility for the Life & Pensions Department expanded in 1965 to running both the Home Non-Marine Department and the UK branch network, which he did with enormous success, as many blue chip companies became clients of the firm. He became a Life Director in 1965.

Ronnie Taylor's four-year tenure as Chairman was brief compared with those of most of his predecessors. On the other hand, while previous Chairmen of Willis might have been known by sight, they were generally distant and remote figures to the great majority of employees. John Roscoe did produce a brief guide for new employees – 'An outline of the Company's history and its activities' – but the occasional communication from the Chair-

Ronnie Taylor

man would generally be by means of a somewhat impersonal letter. Ronnie Taylor believed in taking his message direct to employees. He was doubtless influenced heavily by his army experiences. Maintaining at all times a military bearing and staff officer's precision, he relished addressing staff, whether speaking to a handful in a small branch office or to a large gathering in the Tower Room at Ten Trinity Square or in the restaurant at the top of the Ipswich building. He was a stickler for timekeeping, and woe betide the person who turned up after he had started speaking.

When the Ipswich project was started in the early 1970s, and for a number of years after its completion, trades unions were a

67

more powerful force generally than they are today. Representing Willis employees would have been a considerable coup, and the unions made a determined attempt to do so by picketing the building and recruiting members. Ronnie Taylor was equally determined to keep them out, and he tirelessly and passionately drove home the values and culture of Willis in his speeches to audiences, the majority of whom were recent employees. To this day there is no trades union representation in Ipswich. The company he inherited still had the vestiges of the old partnership structures and culture where Marine had predominated. He instituted a series of far-ranging organisational changes which laid down clear lines of responsibility and accountability. The structure he put in place is one that is broadly in place today.

Strong headwinds accompanied the period of his Chairmanship. A soft market environment in broking reduced income and profits from underwriting, and currency conversion had an adverse impact of £7 million for 1978–80. Pre-tax profits in 1978 were 2.2 per cent lower than 1977. Whilst income rose by 9 per cent, the cost increases predicted in the 1977 report came through. Pre-tax profits declined to £17.2 million in 1979 and then recovered sharply in 1980 to £19.4 million.

Neither Willis Faber nor Johnson & Higgins was an important player in the oil and gas insurance market. What business Willis Faber had was handled by the Marine Division. Donald Payne, recruited from Sedgwick in 1979, formed a separate Oil & Gas Division. This grew very rapidly, and substantial business emanated from the reinsurance broking operation set up jointly with Heddington, Texaco's wholly owned insurance company, in Bermuda in 1981. In the same year a controlling interest was acquired in Carter, Wilkes & Fane, a specialist reinsurance broker.

Ronnie Taylor had to deal with the reputational issues arising from what became known as the Savonita Affair. This achieved a great deal of publicity, much of it ill-informed. On 26 November 1974 the motor vessel *Savonita* left her loading port of Savona, Italy, laden with a cargo of cars owned by Fiat and destined for the United States. Eight hours out she took fire and returned to Savona where 301 cars, damaged as a result of the fire, were unloaded. The cars were insured by Societa Italiana Assicur-azioni e Riassicurazioni (SIAT), at the time Fiat's captive insurer, and reinsured with Lloyd's and Company Underwriters. The unloaded cars were sold by Fiat to a main dealer in Naples for 81 million lire, representing 15 per cent of their market value. Fiat were then paid by SIAT the difference between the declared value of the cars and the proceeds of the sale.

In January 1975 Fiat's cargo brokers, Pearson Webb Spring-bett (PWS) presented a claim to the reinsuring underwriters for US $711,643. This became contentious as PWS suggested that the claim had been inflated. Matters between SIAT and PWS deteriorated, and in April 1976 SIAT replaced them with Willis. John Prentice was intimately involved in all these events through his close personal and professional relationship with Giorgio Mitolo of SIAT.

PWS took legal advice and, at the same time, encouraged underwriters not to settle. They had kept the Chairman of Lloyd's informed of developments. At a meeting with him in November 1977 they sought his assistance to get Willis to withdraw certain alleged defamatory remarks and also to persuade SIAT to allow PWS one month to collect the claim. The Chairman declined to intervene on a claims matter but offered to take up any question of possible misconduct. He then held two meetings with Willis regarding the alleged defamatory remarks.

In February 1978 Malcolm Pearson, Chairman of PWS, wrote to Ronnie Taylor informing him of their intention to issue defamation proceedings. The letter was copied to the Chairman of Lloyd's. While this was happening Willis continued to negotiate the claim. By the end of February 1978 a settlement of US $543,000 had been agreed with all reinsuring underwriters and collected by Willis.

This however, was not the end of the matter. On 23 March 1978 Jonathan Aitken, MP, a contemporary of Malcolm Pearson at Eton and more recently a business associate of his, raised the Savonita issue in an Adjournment Debate in the House of Commons. The Committee of Lloyd's set up a Board of Enquiry, the terms of reference being 'To inquire into and report to the Committee of Lloyd's on all the circumstances concerning the handling of the "SAVONITA" claim as they affect Lloyd's.'

With one minor exception, the Board of Enquiry concluded, in relation to Willis, 'that no criticism can be levelled at them for the manner in which they handled the claim'. The exception was that at one meeting with reinsuring underwriters, 'the behaviour of the WFD personnel concerned was robust beyond the normally acceptable standards of broking conduct'.

Was the Board of Enquiry too lenient on Willis? Some saw it as a case of a large and powerful broker using its muscle to push aside a smaller and bothersome rival and to bully underwriters into paying the claim. 'The report is a shoddy document that smacks heavily of kangaroo justice,' thundered the *Economist*. The report did not mention that Willis had a 4 per cent shareholding in SIAT and that John Prentice sat on the Board of SIAT. In his book *The Business and Battlecry*, Prentice acknowledges that Willis were concerned about Malcolm Pearson's success in penetrating the Fiat account where Willis had long enjoyed a strong position. There was no mention, either, that overtures had been made to Pearson about selling his business to Willis.

Willis staunchly defended their conduct, insisting that they had acted in the best interest of their client and had collected the claim on the well-established principle that as the reassured – SIAT – had settled it, reinsurers were bound to follow.

After three challenging years, 1981 saw more satisfactory results. Pre-tax profits were £27.1 million, broken down as follows:

Insurance Broking	£20.9
Underwriting agencies	£1.6
Sovereign	£1.1
Morgan Grenfell	£3.5
	£27.1 million

Ronnie Taylor retired at the end of 1981 and was succeeded by David Palmer. The split in role of Chairman and Chief Executive was discontinued, but reintroduced with the merger with Corroon & Black nine years later.

CHAPTER SEVEN

---※-0-※---

1982–1987

David Vereker Palmer (1926–) was educated at Stowe School. From there he went, in 1944, to the Royal Military Academy at Sandhurst. Commissioned into the Life Guards, he saw service in Germany, Egypt and Palestine. He left the army in 1949 to join the Lloyd's broking firm of Edward Lumley & Son, and in 1954 was transferred to their New York office, where he spent the next five years. In 1959 he was recruited by Elwyn Rhys and Julian Faber to join Willis's American Department. He rose rapidly, appointed an Ordinary Director in 1961 and a Life Director in 1965. Following the retirement of Guy Wilson he was given responsibility for Finance, Administration and Human Resources. He became Deputy Chairman in 1972, Chief Executive in 1978, and finally Chairman in 1982, serving for two months short of seven years, a longer term than anyone since Elwyn Rhys. His first five years were certainly exciting as well as successful ones.

The management structure had become much more formalised under Ronnie Taylor and covered four areas of activity – international broking, overseas operations, domestic broking and underwriting. These activities were controlled by five principal subsidiaries:

1 Willis Faber & Dumas, which incorporated all the international broking divisions
2 Willis Faber & Dumas UK, which handled non-marine business

David Palmer

within the United Kingdom together with the regional branch network, employee benefits and Hughes Gibb, the specialist bloodstock
company
3 Willis Faber International, which was concerned with the overseas
subsidiaries and relationships with associated companies abroad
4 Willis Faber Underwriting Management, which underwrote in London on behalf of British and overseas insurance companies, including
the subsidiary, Sovereign Marine & General
5 Willis Faber Agencies, which acted as underwriting agents at Lloyd's,
managed syndicates in all classes of business and looked after the
interest of Names.

Pre-tax profits were £32.4 million in 1982. By 1986 they had increased to £74.8 million. During this period the contribution of Morgan Grenfell increased from £6 million to £18.1 million. Running alongside, but separate from, Willis Faber Underwriting Management, Devonport Underwriting Agency Limited (DUAL) started business in Autumn 1982, underwriting a Non-Marine Account in the London market on behalf of four companies, including the wholly-owned Devonport Insurance Company.

There were substantial changes to both the composition and structure of the Board in the first five years of David Palmer's Chairmanship. Marine had dominated the firm for most of its history. Its decline relative to Reinsurance over the decades was inexorable and painful to some. Chris Hughes resigned in March 1982. This, coupled with John Prentice having become a non-executive Director, signalled the end of the old Marine ascendancy. Edward Gumbel and Tommy Thomson, head of the UK business, both retired at the end of 1983.

Edward Gumbel continued to act as a consultant to Willis, as well as retaining a number of appointments with companies traditionally associated with the firm. Deserved honours followed. In 1984 he was decorated with the Commander's Cross of the Order of Merit of the Federal Republic of Germany, and in 1989 he was appointed OBE. At his death in 1995 his obituary in *The Times* noted that during his long professional career he became probably the best-known reinsurance broker in the world. He was also paid this tribute by John Prentice in his book: 'If Douglas-Whyte had laid the foundations of the Reinsurance Department, it was Edward who designed and put together the fabric of the building, though he had much help from Dick Bowes from the mid-sixties onwards.'

Kenneth Childs, a Deputy Chairman who had built the highly

Edward Gumbel

successful International Division and who had a particularly
strong relationship with Johnson & Higgins, died in 1984 after a
brief illness. Bill Mackworth-Young, Chairman of Morgan Grenfell and a non-executive Director of Willis, died in the same year.
John Robins joined the firm in February 1984 as Group Finance
Director, having previously held a similar role at Fitch Lovell.
Jeremy Cohen, Derek Shaw, Donald Payne and John Wooderson
were all appointed to the Board in the same year and in 1986
were joined by Ray Salter.

The Lloyd's Act 1982 required the divestment by brokers of
their Lloyd's Managing Agency interests. Willis Faber & Dumas
Agencies looked after the interests of around 850 members of

Lloyd's and managed nine Lloyd's syndicates. John Prentice had retired from the Board to become Chairman of the divested Lloyd's underwriting business, leaving Allan Sykes and Charles Rawlinson as the remaining non-executive Directors. They were joined in September 1985 by Lord Pennock, a distinguished industrialist, and Michael Rendle, a former Managing Director of BP. In March 1986 it was announced that David Palmer would continue as Chairman and Chief Executive beyond his normal retirement date of 31 December 1986.

There was considerable activity in the United States. In furtherance of its relationship with Johnson & Higgins, and to get on-the-ground earnings, a 49 per cent interest was acquired in Willcox Incorporated Reinsurance Intermediaries in 1983, Johnson & Higgins having 51 per cent. This went alongside the 40 per cent interest held in Neal Lloyd & Co. This Chicago-based company, of which Johnson & Higgins owned 60 per cent, had evolved from its surplus lines origin into a specialist marketing organisation for large clients. A more far-reaching deal was concluded in 1984 with the acquisition of Global Special Risks, a surplus line agent in New Orleans specialising in the oil and gas industry. This was driven by Donald Payne. It was the first time Willis had entered the United States without Johnson & Higgins. They were, though, one of the principal producers of business for Global Special Risks. In 1986 McLear Associates, a surplus line broker operating principally in Grand Rapids, Michigan, was acquired by Willis.

Closer to home, the remaining minority share in Carter, Wilkes & Fane was purchased in 1982 following the acquisition of a controlling interest in October of the previous year. A specialist reinsurance broker, they operated independently for a number of years.

The year 1986 marked a decade since Willis's floatation on the

Stock Exchange. Pre-tax profits that year were £74.8 million, of which insurance broking contributed £57 million. In retrospect, 1986 was the end of an era for the firm. The aura surrounding its fabled reputation with clients and markets globally was progressively fading, with increasing competition from rival brokers both in London and around the world. Perhaps, also, a measure of complacency and a sense of entitlement had set in.

CHAPTER EIGHT

A New Wife and an Old Mistress

On 29 June 1987 Willis announced an agreed merger with their smaller rival, Stewart Wrightson Holdings plc. Willis at the time employed around 4,000 people, while Stewart Wrightson employed around 2,700. Stewart Wrightson had a distinguished history. James Woodrow Matthews had started his business career in his native Devon, moving to London to work for the shipping firm William Lamplough & Co., where he eventually became head of their Lloyd's Department. Harry Wrightson worked as an insurance broker for his cousin Ernest Cooper, a firm that eventually became Hartley Cooper & Co. Ltd. Matthews and Wrightson went into partnership in February 1901 and the new firm was known as Matthews Wrightson & Co., described in the partnership deed as 'Ship and Insurance Brokers or Agents'. They were incorporated as a limited company in 1911 and James Matthews became Chairman. In January 1971 they merged with Bray Gibb and later that year floated on the London Stock Exchange. In 1972 they merged with Stewart Smith, when the business became known as Stewart Wrightson.

Bray Gibb pioneered aviation insurance at Lloyd's before the First World War and went on to develop business from both Europe and the United States. Their clients included such famous names as Bleriot, Bristol, Vickers and Sopwith. Stewart Smith was formed in 1936 from the amalgamation of Stewart Flint and Fletcher & Smith. This firm had been built largely on a highly successful direct aviation account.

The merger was an all-stock transaction whereby Stewart Wrightson shareholders received three Willis shares for every two they held. This valued Stewart Wrightson at around £300 million. Stewart Wrightson's pre-tax profits in 1986 were £21.52 million. It was generally felt that Stewart Wrightson had obtained a full price. As this was an agreed merger, limited due diligence was undertaken. With the decline of the Willis share price between the announcement of the merger and its completion, the cost of the acquisition ended up at £253 million.

Willis had made smaller bolt-on acquisitions, including Durtnell & Fowler – who brought both Hughes Gibb, the bloodstock business, and the prized Municipal Mutual reinsurance account – and the reinsurance broker Carter, Wilkes & Fane in London. It had also made various smaller acquisitions of UK provincial brokers. Willis had also, over the years, flirted with C. T. Bowring, J. H. Minet and Hogg Robinson without ever consummating a deal. The merger with Stewart Wrightson, which was completed on 28 August 1987, was by far the largest that Willis had ever attempted. The benefits of the merger were explained as follows:

1 reinforcing the position as a leading British-based independent international insurance broker
2 substantially increasing the base of UK retail business and thus improving the balance with the wholesale and reinsurance portfolio
3 producing better overall profits than each company could produce separately
4 strengthening the service to clients both in the range of specialities and an increased geographical coverage
5 providing the ability to handle an increased volume of business with a reduction in the ratio of overheads and administrative costs to revenue.

David Palmer noted, 'There is no middle ground in insurance broking.' What was not stated, but was clearly implicit, was that David Rowland, Chairman of Stewart Wrightson and now Deputy Chairman of Willis Faber, would succeed David Palmer.

Stewart Wrightson brought with them the Stewart Smith surplus line business in the United States and Canada, thereby increasing dollar earnings in the United States. They also brought a strong UK retail business, a renowned capability in the field of professional indemnity and a strong financial institutions client base. There was also a retail business in Portugal. Whilst the rationale for the merger made good business sense it was not always matched by decisive execution. It also became clear very early on that the cultures of the two firms were markedly different, and there was ambiguity as to whether it was a merger or a takeover. The upshot was that large numbers of Stewart Wrightson employees decided to pursue their careers elsewhere, some moving to competitors and others starting up their own businesses. Aviation presented particular challenges which proved intractable. Nicholson Stewart Wrightson, a Lloyd's aviation reinsurance broker, was 51 per cent owned by Stewart Wrightson and 49 per cent by three Directors. Willis was unable to come to an agreement with these Directors for the purchase of their shares and the retention of their services. There was inevitably a haemorrhaging of business from these defections. The position on business from the United States also presented difficulties. Willis, of course, worked with Johnson & Higgins, whilst Nicholson Stewart Wrightson sourced business from both Rollins Burdick and Frank Crystal. This situation was simply not acceptable to Johnson & Higgins.

Dick Bowes had joined Willis from the G. N. Rouse Syndicate at Lloyd's in 1966 and was made a Life Director. With Edward Gumbel, he had developed the reinsurance business to its eminent market position. He retired from the Board as Deputy Chairman at the end of 1987. At the start of 1988 there were twenty Directors, five of whom had come from Stewart Wrightson. Within three years only Alan Gregory, a non-executive Director, remained from Stewart Wrightson.

With the completion of the merger the Board turned its attention to who should succeed David Palmer. Allen Sykes, a non-executive Director who had previously been an Executive Director of Willis, canvassed the Board. In March 1988 the Board announced that Roger Elliott would succeed David Palmer as Chairman. The decisive factor that counted against David Rowland was the set of disappointments arising from the merger. David Rowland, the co-architect of the merger, resigned to become Chief Executive and subsequently Chairman of Sedgwick, a great rival of Willis. *The Times* of 12 March 1988 observed, 'Mr Rowland's surprise move comes after a spate of departures by former SW staff in what has proved to be a bloody merger, despite its friendly intent.' He went on to become an outstanding Chairman of Lloyd's, where he will be best remembered for what was termed Reconstruction and Renewal. This put an end to market-wide litigation and drew a line under massive losses by reinsuring the 1992 and prior year business underwritten by its members (Names) into Equitas, a UK authorised reinsurer. He was knighted in 1997. David Palmer, the other co-architect of the merger, retired at the end of October 1988 after thirty years of distinguished service to the firm.

Roger John Elliott (1933–) was educated at Brighton College. An accomplished rugby and cricket player, he was prevented by a sporting injury from doing military service. He joined the American Department, and was subsequently attached to Johnson & Higgins on the West Coast of America from 1963 to 1965. On his return he went to the Marine Hull Department, working with Henry Dumas and Jack White. He became a Life Director in 1972 and in 1979 took over the leadership of the Aviation Division from Henry White-Smith. He was appointed a Deputy Chairman to Dick Bowes following the Stewart Wrightson merger. On becoming Chairman he set himself a number of objectives, of which the most important were to:

1 address the future of the Ten Trinity Square head office building
2 resolve the Morgan Grenfell shareholding
3 strengthen the Johnson & Higgins relationship.

Although Ten Trinity Square was a splendid and prestigious head office it was not a particularly efficient building, and it was quite unsuitable for the new communications technology. The choices came down to sell, refurbish or redevelop. The Board decided upon refurbishment and capital approval was given. This proved extraordinarily expensive. The total cost was around £30 million, and this had a serious impact on cash flow between 1992 and 1994.

In late 1989 Banque Indosuez made an offer for the Willis 20.4 per cent interest in Morgan Grenfell. Just over half the holding was sold at 410p per share with an option to sell the balance at 462p per share. Prior to completion, a substantially better offer of 550p per share was made by Deutsche Bank for the whole of Morgan Grenfell. This marked a highly profitable exit for Willis from an investment made over twenty years earlier. It was also a satisfactory outcome for the employees of Morgan Grenfell, who no longer had the uncertainty associated with a substantial minority shareholder.

The relationship with Johnson & Higgins was a constant preoccupation of successive Chairmen of Willis. The personal chemistry between the respective Chairmen was pivotal. For most of the almost 100-year association this was generally very good, and the inevitable odd spat was dealt with swiftly and without rancour. This was perhaps less so with Richard I. Purnell, Chairman of Johnson & Higgins between 1972 and 1981. He was an abrasive character whose sobriquet was appropriately 'The Ripper'.

The relationship had prospered with the exclusive agreement in relation to marine hull business. Over the years, considerable volumes of non-marine business which had been produced by the Johnson & Higgins office network across the United States were placed by Willis in the London market. Willis was also the beneficiary of business from the UK subsidiaries of US multinational clients of Johnson & Higgins. After the Second World War both firms broadened their activities. Lex Douglas-Whyte and Edward Gumbel energetically developed international reinsurance business whilst Johnson & Higgins focused upon building a global retail network to serve their multinational clients. Willis supported Johnson & Higgins by putting their retail operations in Canada, Australia and New Zealand into jointly held companies. They were also supportive in helping Johnson & Higgins put together the European retail network, which was to be branded UNISON. With the exception of Italy, which Johnson & Higgins had built up from scratch, all members apart from Willis had strong family ownership ties. Chief among them were Gil y Carvajel in Spain, Gras Savoye in France and Jauch & Hübener in Germany.

The first serious crack in the relationship came when Willis went public in 1976. As already mentioned, there was no consultation with Johnson & Higgins, who were aggrieved and also alarmed at the possibility of Willis's being acquired by a competitor. The acquisition of Global Special Risks in 1984 and Mclear Associates in 1986 represented an incursion by Willis onto US soil. Whilst not competing directly with Johnson & Higgins, it was done without their acquiescence. The merger with Stewart Wrightson was seen as a show of force by Willis, and the inclusion of the Stewart Smith surplus lines business expanded their footprint in the United States. Reflecting their own ambitions, in 1987 Johnson & Higgins acquired the small London reinsurance broker, Carter Brito & Cunha Ltd, which had been founded by two former Willis employees. Willis for its part saw this as a Trojan horse.

Both sides were aware of the resultant strains in the relationship, and high-level conferences were held to identify and resolve these. The first, dubbed London Bridge I, was held in New York in 1986, and London Bridge II took place in London the following year. These were by no means the earliest discussions. During Ronnie Taylor's tenure there had been a get-together at the Carlyle Hotel in New York, known as the Atlantic Charter meeting. Various options were examined, including the establishment of a joint holding company to overcome the impediment of a publicly traded company, Willis, merging with a private partnership, Johnson & Higgins.

The appointment of Bob Hatcher as Richard Purnell's successor as Chairman of Johnson & Higgins provided some impetus. He and David Palmer enjoyed an excellent personal and professional relationship and they wanted to achieve closer business ties between the two firms. Bob Hatcher favoured both bringing in outside capital to Johnson & Higgins and a merger with Willis. He was unable, though, to get his fellow-Directors to support either course of action. In 1989 Roger Elliott and Bob Hatcher put together a negotiating team comprising four Board members from each firm. The discussions covered a well-trodden path, and could be summed up as what a former Director of Johnson & Higgins described as a tussle over 'whose flag would be at the top of the pole'.

Fifty per cent of the World's non-life insurance premiums emanated from the United States, and in order to grow Willis needed more direct access to this market. Plainly, Johnson & Higgins would not allow this to happen. For their part, Johnson & Higgins, who needed access to the London market, looked enviously at Willis's great international wholesale and reinsurance business where they were, at best, marginal players. Japan was a particular area of friction. Johnson & Higgins had started a business there in 1968 and invested heavily in it. The great insurance companies such as Tokio Marine and Taisho Marine, however, looked more readily to their long-term advisers, Willis.

The Johnson & Higgins proposal was that they would run retail globally, international wholesale and the specialisms. Willis would run reinsurance. This would have given Johnson & Higgins effective control without paying for it, and was not a proposition that the Board of Willis could put to their shareholders. In reality, Johnson & Higgins could not buy Willis as they had limited capital in their partnership structure and a large proportion of the annual profits was being paid to retired Directors.

At that time Adrian Gregory ran the Willis UK retail business, and he was strongly opposed to Johnson & Higgins taking over its management. He was probably one of the more strategic thinkers on the Willis Board and it was he who reiterated the need for Willis to have a Plan B. In February 1990 discussions were initiated with the US firm Corroon & Black Corporation.

CHAPTER NINE

Corroon & Black and the Johnson
& Higgins Divorce

Corroon & Black was incorporated in Delaware in 1928 under the name of Corroon & Reynolds Corporation. In 1929 its stock was listed on the American Stock Exchange. The business had been founded in New York as the R. A. Corroon Company as an insurance broker and agent. Through the early 1960s the company's primary focus was on the management and control of a number of small insurance companies and agencies, although a small brokerage operation was maintained. In 1964 it sold its insurance companies and embarked upon a programme of growth in insurance broking, with the goal of becoming a national business. In 1966 it acquired the C. R. Black Corporation and in 1968 changed its name to Corroon & Black Corporation. Thereafter it grew, primarily through over a hundred acquisitions, from a company with $113 million of revenue in 1965 to one with revenues of $491 million in 1989. The acquisition of Nashville-based Synercon in 1976 was, at the time, the largest ever in the United States.

Corroon & Black had no material revenues outside the United State. Recognising the need to expand from their domestic base, in 1975 they acquired a 35 per cent interest in Glanvill Enthoven, a well-respected medium-sized UK-based insurance broking firm. In 1979 they acquired a 20 per cent holding in Minet, a much more substantial UK insurance broking firm which was about the same size as Corroon & Black. This holding was later increased to 29.9 per cent, and the goal was to arrange a merger of the two companies. This was frustrated in 1988 when St Paul, a large American insurance company, acquired Minet.

The management of Corroon & Black then engaged Booz Allen & Hamilton, an international consulting firm, to assist them in an examination of the company's strategic objectives for the 1990s. This culminated in the adoption of Plan 95, which included as one of its primary objectives the re-establishment of an international presence, particularly in the globally significant London market. Plan 95 called for the acquisition of a major UK retail broker and one or more major reinsurance brokers, and for revenues from international operations to constitute at least 20 per cent of the total by 1995. Corroon & Black actively set about implementing this plan and had acquisition discussions with several British and continental European brokers. However, all the proposed transactions posed serious business and financial risks, particularly because asking prices were high in relation to earnings and this would have resulted in a substantial dilution of Corroon & Black's earnings per share.

On 19 February 1990 Corroon & Black and Willis Faber executed a confidentiality agreement and the two companies exchanged information about their respective businesses. Discussions took place over the next few months with senior executives from both sides, together with their respective legal and financial advisers. Extensive due diligence was undertaken by both parties. Corroon & Black were particularly concerned at Willis's underwriting activities whilst Willis were concerned about the financial commitment of the new Corroon & Black Nashville headquarters. Both sets of concerns proved prescient.

Corroon & Black had over a hundred offices throughout the United States, working through three operating groups: retail broking (with a strong presence in the middle market); a whole-

Roger Elliott with Dick Miller

saler and administrator of insurance programmes and an employee benefit consultant; and a reinsurance intermediary. In
1989 revenues were $439 million and net income $33 million.
Richard Miller was Chairman and Chief Executive.

On 4 June 1990 the merger was announced, with the new
company to be named Willis Corroon plc. The terms of the deal
involved Corroon & Black shareholders receiving 7.8 Willis
shares for each Corroon & Black share. Before the announcement
the shares traded as $36.50 and £2.91 respectively. The trans-
action closed on 8 October 1990. The Board of Directors was

drawn equally from both firms. Roger Elliott became Executive Chairman and Richard Miller became Chief Executive.

The decision to effectively sever the Johnson & Higgins relationship was arguably the most momentous that a Chairman of Willis had ever had to make. It was particularly painful for Roger Elliott who had, through his long career, forged close business relationships with Johnson & Higgins. It stunned employees of both firms, many of whom had built their careers on developing and serving mutual clients. It was also a massive surprise to the outside world, particularly competitors, who had long looked enviously at what they saw as a successful and enduring relationship. What they did not see were the strains that had developed over many years. In May 1990 virtually the entire Johnson & Higgins senior management team had gone to London for three days to increase the firm's visibility in the London market, and on the last night Willis gave a farewell dinner at the Imperial War Museum. A number of Willis people in fact knew this really was farewell and not merely *auf Wiedersehen.*

Johnson & Higgins had a ready-made operation, Carter Brito, through which to channel wholesale business, although it required a substantial increase in its resources. For retail business they first looked at acquiring a UK firm, but eventually decided to set up an operation from scratch. Offices were opened in London, Birmingham, Glasgow, Manchester, Newcastle, Reading and Dublin, trading as Johnson & Higgins UK Limited.

Both firms had pledged to keep the interest of clients uppermost, and no business was transferred from Willis to Johnson & Higgins without the client's approval. Over time, the majority of business was transferred in a professional manner. Johnson & Higgins sold their shareholding in Willis. The international relationships were also unwound, with Willis buying out the Johnson & Higgins shareholding in Australia and New Zealand

and Johnson & Higgins buying out the Willis shareholding in Canada. There is no escaping, however, that the end of the relationship was sad and sometimes acrimonious, though in retrospect the decision was not so surprising. Perhaps the most apposite comment came from Don Carlson, manager of the Johnson & Higgins office in St Louis, who said, 'We had a long relationship and it was a good one. That's what should be emphasised, not the rancour of the final few months. We did a lot with them, and our clients benefited.'

The year 1995 marked the 150th since the founding of Johnson & Higgins. By this time it was apparent that they had lost a considerable amount of ground to their two great rivals, Marsh & McLennan and Aon. They brought in both McKinsey and Morgan Stanley to review the competitive environment and to consider options, which included going public and selling to another broker. On 12 March 1997 Johnson & Higgins announced the sale of the firm to their long-time arch rivals, Marsh & McLennan, for $1.8 billion, representing one-and-a-half times revenue. This was a seismic event on the same scale as the divorce from Willis. When the deal was completed the proceeds were divided 50 per cent to the Directors, 25 per cent to key employees and 25 per cent to former Directors. The Directors all became extraordinarily rich through selling 150 years of goodwill, just as the Willis Faber Directors had done in 1976, the difference being, of course, that in the case of Willis Faber it was the shares in the firm that were put on the market, not the firm itself.

The business of Johnson & Higgins was rapidly absorbed into the Marsh empire. Many people left, its identity was lost, and a venerable name in the history of insurance, as well as the UNISON brand, disappeared. The great European broking firms of Jauch & Hübener and Gil y Carjavel were sold to Aon, whilst Gras Savoye sold a share of their business to Willis.

CHAPTER TEN

A Brave New World

The merger with Corroon & Black was embraced enthusiastically and there was goodwill on both sides to make it work. Dick Miller headed the Transition Committee. Early on, though, there were misunderstandings. So far as the Brits were concerned, Roger Elliott as Executive Chairman was in charge. For the Americans, it was Dick Miller as Chief Executive. Hence there were duplicated functions in London and Nashville. This ambiguous situation was never satisfactorily resolved. Notwithstanding detailed due diligence and extensive contact at senior level, there was a fundamental misunderstanding between the respective firms. Willis imagined that Corroon & Black would be like Johnson & Higgins and Corroon & Black expected Willis to be like Minet. This produced a mutual mismatch of expectations and inevitable disappointments which took many years to reverse.

One of the earliest initiatives was the opening of a representative office in Tokyo in November 1990. This highly significant move was made with strong encouragement from the firm's Japanese clients. To reflect the importance of the development Henry White-Smith transferred to Tokyo to become head of the office, and a glittering opening party was held, attended by the most prestigious clients. Two years later the office began operating a non-life agency, and in 1996 it became the first international broker to achieve a full broking licence.

A much more sombre development occurred in 1991, when

the Board made the decision to withdraw from underwriting, an activity in which the firm had been prominently engaged for well over a hundred years. At that time Willis Faber Underwriting Management was underwriting principally on behalf of Tokio Marine, Taisho (later renamed Mitsui), Allianz, Heddington (a subsidiary of Texaco), Storebrand and the wholly-owned Sovereign. They were known collectively as 'stamp' companies. The decision was made for two reasons. First, a number of the companies had ambitions to become more prominent in the London market and to underwrite on their own account. Secondly, the 'stamp' companies had incurred significant losses, particularly from disease claims emanating from business underwritten many years earlier. The intention was to have an orderly run-off of the business, estimated at twenty-five years, and a provision of £55 million was made to cover losses. Further provisions were made in 1995 and 1997.

The withdrawal from the UNISON network led by Johnson & Higgins necessitated the building of a replacement international network, and this was achieved by a variety of acquisitions and start-ups. Over a five-year period Willis focused extensively on Europe. It also opened offices in South Korea, Brunei, Peru, Mexico, Taiwan, Venezuela and Canada. A substantial investment in building specialist businesses also took place in the United States, chiefly in the areas of aerospace, energy and reinsurance.

These investments were usually made in advance of achieving revenue streams, and the substantial costs took a heavy toll on profits. In 1991, the first full year of the merged business, pre-tax profits were £96.1 million. This slipped to £42.5 million in 1992 (after a loss of £25.7 million attributable to discontinued UK underwriting) and the dividend was reduced. A recovery in pre-tax profits to £76.2 million in 1993 was followed in 1994 by a further setback with pre-tax profits of £57.4 million, £17 million less than Willis Faber had achieved alone in 1986, prior to the Stewart Wrightson and Corroon & Black mergers. Plainly, something had to be done, and a strategic review was undertaken. This concluded that after the merger too much had been attempted, in too many locations, and too quickly.

Group operations were restructured into five business segments: UK retail, North American retail, US wholesale, international, and global specialties such as aerospace and reinsurance. The restructuring was accompanied by cost savings, involving the elimination of 800 jobs worldwide, office closures and property disposals. This gave rise to a £49 million exceptional items charge against 1994 profits. Resulting cost savings were predicted at £26 million in 1995 rising to £39 million annually thereafter. Pre-tax profits recovered to £79 million in 1995. Whilst operating revenue at £706 million was unchanged, operating expenses were cut through a further 10 per cent reduction in worldwide staff numbers and the balance sheet gearing ratio sharply reduced.

Over a three-year period the principal architects of the merger left the stage. Adrian Gregory and Jake Wallace retired in 1993. Bob Corroon died in 1994; in the same year John Robins resigned to become Chief Executive of Guardian Royal Exchange and Dick Miller stepped down as Chief Executive, although he stayed on the Board as Vice Chairman. Both Roger Elliott and Dick Miller retired at the end of 1995, and John Reeve became Executive Chairman on 1 December that year.

CHAPTER ELEVEN

Reconstruction and Tribulations

John Reeve (1944–) was educated at Westcliff High School. He qualified as a chartered accountant and spent some time with Peat Marwick, now part of KPMG. Moving into industry, he had spells at Roneo Vickers, Wilkinson Match, Amalgamated Metal and British Aluminium. Prior to being headhunted to join Willis he had spent five years as Group Managing Director of Sun Life Assurance. He was the first Chairman of Willis to be appointed from outside, in a clear demonstration by the Board that a fresh approach was needed to address the firm's challenges, unencumbered by history and ingrained attitudes. He quickly recognised that there was no clear strategy and that the marriage to Corroon & Black had not healed the scars from the Johnson & Higgins divorce.

A fundamental review of strategy was initiated both at business unit and group level. John Reeve concluded that Willis lacked sufficicent staff with the experience to lead major operational change, and McKinsey, the global management consulting firm, was brought in to provide advice and expertise. This in-volved a large number of projects, staffed by both McKinsey consultants and Willis secondees, addressing, in particular, the re-engineering of processes.

Two major outcomes resulted. First, the strategy was articulated, in a booklet entitled 'Our New Vision', as seeking leadership positions in those market segments where the firm chose to

John Reeve

operate. Second, a group-wide change programme was introduced to import working practices proven in other industries.
This was in order to achieve best practice and aimed to move the
firm from being a traditional insurance broker to becoming a
global knowledge-based professional services firm. This work,
and the involvement of McKinsey, lasted throughout John
Reeve's Chairmanship. The strategic focus resulted in the dis-
posal of a number of activities no longer considered core to the
business; these included W. F. Corroon (the global employee
benefits consulting business), the Lloyd's Members Agency and

Consumer Benefit Life (a US life insurance company). The proceeds from these disposals were recycled in the business with continuing investment in the global network, notably in France, Germany, Italy, Chile, Norway, Argentina, Mexico and Venezuela. France represented the largest investment, with the acquisition of 33 per cent of Gras Savoye, the other shareholders being the Gras and Savoye families, some insurance companies and the executive management team. There was also an increase in the existing shareholdings in Sweden, Netherlands, Australia and Spain, which had significant minority shareholders.

In 1997 pre-tax profits rose to £91.6 million, the highest ever. The firm had 11,000 employees worldwide and handled £7 billion in premiums, but there were unwelcome, and costly, distractions from achieving the benefits of the change programme. These can be summarised as underwriting and pensions mis-selling. The orderly Sovereign run-off was rudely interrupted in 1997 when it became involved in a dispute with Axa over a £12 million reinsurance claim which went to arbitration. There was great concern that the point on which the arbitration would be decided would be used by other reinsurers of both Sovereign and the 'stamp' companies. The implications of this for the firm were unquantifiable and the decision was made to put Sovereign into provisional liquidation, with KPMG appointed as provisional liquidators and, subsequently, scheme administrators.

Richard Bucknall was, at the time, managing the highly successful Global Specialties business unit. He was then also awarded responsibility for Willis Faber Underwriting Management, including managing sensitive relationships in the run-off of the 'stamp' companies. Whilst this was a messy chapter in the history of the firm, the overall outcome could have been far worse. Litigation was largely avoided, the run-off was seen to be orderly and a successful scheme of arrangement was ultimately sanctioned by the courts. This took several years to resolve, at the end of which the whole sorry saga had cost Willis at least £100 million. The US professional liability wholesale operation (PLUM) was also closed in May 1998. This led to a £29.6 million write-off.

Within Willis UK an independent financial advisory services business operated out of both London and the branch offices around the country. In August 1997 the formation of Willis National was announced, a joint venture between Abbey National and Willis Corroon Financial Planning to create the second largest independent financial adviser in the United Kingdom. This became fully operational in January 1998, with Willis having a 51 per cent shareholding and Abbey 49 per cent.

Concern had been growing over many years that some financial advisers, in selling pension plans to individuals, had put personal enrichment ahead of giving best advice. The more egregious cases were frequently highlighted in the media, and the term 'pensions mis-selling' was coined. The consequence was that Willis Corroon Financial Planning, along with all other financial advisers, were required by the Financial Services Authority and the Personal Investment Authority to review certain categories of personal pension plans sold to individuals between 1988 and 1994. They were required to compensate individuals who transferred from, opted out of, or did not join, their employer-sponsored pension plan if the expected benefits from the pension plan which they had been sold did not equal the benefits that would have been available from their employer-sponsored pension plan. An initial amount of £500,000 was set aside to provide compensation. This was rapidly increased to £5 million; the expectation that this would be more than adequate was to prove optimistic, as the provisions increased progressively. The final cost was £65 million. To put this in context, the Willis

Financial Planning business typically made annual profits of less than £1 million.

At the time it was believed that there could be no recovery from the professional indemnity insurers. Several years later a claim was made, the argument being that this was a case of systemic failure rather than a series of individual losses, each of which would be subject to an excess. The argument succeeded, and the majority of the £65 million was recovered from these insurers.

CHAPTER TWELVE

---※·◦·※---

Industry Mergers

The day-to-day management of the business and the focus on operational issues was conducted against the backdrop of poor industry fundamentals and a predicted consolidation amongst the largest brokers. Industry consolidation was not new, and there had been a great deal of merger activity already between both small and medium-sized brokers. Among the larger brokers, Marsh had acquired London-based Bowring in 1980, and in the same year Combined International Corporation acquired Chicago-based Rollins Burdick Hunter (Combined was renamed Aon in 1987). Alexander & Alexander acquired Toronto-based Reed Stenhouse in 1985, having earlier acquired London-based Alexander Howden. Willis had, of course, participated in the consolidation process with the Stewart Wrightson merger in 1987 and the Corroon & Black merger in 1990. This series of transactions, plus a host of smaller ones in North America and Europe, resulted in six competing global firms: Alexander & Alexander, Aon, Johnson & Higgins, Marsh, Sedgwick and Willis. At the start of the major consolidation process this was reduced to four when, in 1996, Aon bought Alexander & Alexander and, in 1997, Marsh bought Johnson & Higgins. This left Sedgwick and Willis vulnerable.

The Willis Board were, of course, concerned about these developments. They considered a number of strategic options, including:

1 continuing independence as a public company
2 possible mergers with or acquisition of or by major competitors
3 possible business combinations or strategic alliances with or investments by insurance companies and other financial services companies
   not then engaged in insurance broking.

At various times discussions were held with Alexander & Alexander, Marsh and Sedgwick. A merger with Sedgwick held the
obvious attraction that it would create a British firm large enough
to take on the two American behemoths, Aon and Marsh. Discussions were initiated by John Reeve shortly after Marsh had
acquired Johnson & Higgins. He proposed to Sax Riley, his coun-
terpart at Sedgwick, the setting up of a small group of senior
executives from each firm to examine both the benefits and dis-
advantages of a merger. If this demonstrated a significant net
benefit then a merger should be considered by both boards. Sax
Riley came back and said that he would only agree to setting up a
study group if the key top jobs in the merged business were
agreed in advance. It rapidly became clear that he expected the
roles of Chairman, Chief Executive and Finance Director to fall to
Sedgwick executives. This would have been seen as a takeover
rather than a merger of equals. John Reeve insisted upon having
the merger benefits study first; if this demonstrated substantial
benefits to shareholders the issue of key appointments should be
the responsibility of the Non-Executive Directors of both firms.
Sax Riley would not accept this and shortly afterwards discussions were discontinued.

Following the failure of the merger discussions with Sedgwick, John Reeve pursued a number of initiatives and in the
latter part of 1997 had reached the stage of working with the then
Chase Manhattan Bank with a view to taking the firm private
through a buyout. Then in December 1997 he received a phone

call from Andrew Galloway of HSBC Investment Bank to say that two senior executives of Kohlberg Kravis Roberts (KKR) were in London and would like to have a preliminary discussion on a management buyout.

KKR was founded in 1976 as a private equity firm. It achieved worldwide recognition when in 1989 it won an epic battle to buy RJR Nabisco in what was then the largest buyout in history. Such was the notoriety of this acquisition that it spawned both a book and a film, *Barbarians at the Gate*.

Whether KKR had got wind that Willis was considering a buyout or whether they had already been looking at this independently is debatable. Either way, John Reeve and Tom Colraine, who had succeeded Richard Dalzell as Finance Director, met Perry Golkin from KKR and Jim Fisher, who worked with KKR on insurance matters, along with Andrew Galloway of HSBC. At this exploratory meeting, which covered a wide range of issues, John Reeve indicated the minimum price he felt might be acceptable to his Board, one at a significant premium to the prevailing share price.

Shortly after this meeting, John Reeve flew to New York for discussions involving Henry Kravis and George Roberts, two of the KKR co-founders. This would be their first non-asset backed transaction where 'all of the assets of the firm go home in the elevator at night'. John Reeve was insistent with KKR that in order to make the deal succeed it would be necessary to incentivise around 350 staff, compared with the six or eight who would usually be incentivised in a buyout. He also proposed that a number of insurance companies be involved in the financing, arguing that they would have a vested interest in the continuing independence of a global non-US broker. This subsequently became a condition of the deal.

KKR undertook detailed due diligence. Their particular concerns, unsurprisingly, focused upon Willis Faber Underwriting Management/Sovereign issues and pensions mis-selling. During this time John Reeve spent several months persuading insurance companies to participate. On 22 July 1998 an agreed deal was announced whereby Trinity Acquisitions, a vehicle formed by KKR, offered £2 a share, valuing the Willis equity at £851 million. The transaction was to be financed by KKR, five insurance companies and, of course, a heavy burden of debt. The five insurance companies were GRE (later acquired by AXA), RSA, Chubb, Hartford and Travelers. Tokio Marine joined subsequently.

Given the very large number of people who were aware of the deal it was remarkable that no leak occurred. It probably helped that rumours in both the market and the media over other possible mergers served as a useful smokescreen.

The Board of Willis recommended the deal and gave the following reasons:

1 the share price performance of Willis Corroon over the last few years – the shares had not traded at 200 pence per share since May 1994
2 the offer price represented a premium of 29 per cent over the average closing price of a Willis Corroon share over the previous six months
3 the competitive nature of the insurance broking market, the extent of the restructuring and change which the Willis Corroon Group would have to undertake in order to develop within this environment and the implications for Willis Corroon's share price if Willis Corroon were to remain as an independent listed company
4 the benefits of removing the uncertainty surrounding the future ownership of Willis Corroon for employees, clients and insurance markets
5 the likelihood of the proposed transaction being completed, based on KKR's experience and reputation and the financial resources available to Trinity

6   in the absence of the offer, the doubtful prospects for enhancing shareholder value over the short to medium term.

The day after the deal was announced the *Financial Times* Lex column ran this article under the heading 'Brokering an escape':

Few tears will be shed over the departure of insurance broker Willis Corroon from the London market. Investors were fed up with its under-performance and wary of an industry where competition had ravaged premiums. The US-based market leaders, Marsh & McLennan and Aon, had responded by gobbling up smaller competitors. They are now in a strong position to win the juicier business of providing specialist services to multinational clients.

Investors hoped that Willis would merge with its UK-based rival Sedgwick, or be taken over. This would have made sense in terms of cutting costs and bolstering premiums. But management opposition has unfortunately acted like a poison pill, raising the prospect of an exodus of revenue earners. Insurance company clients would have been alarmed too – no wonder five of them are backing a deal that keeps Willis independent.

But here lies a clue to the decent story that Willis should have told the market. It offers an alternative to the big two in an industry where consolidation must at last swing some power back towards the brokers. Cost cutting should also keep Willis's operating profits rising; at less than 10 times this year's expected figure, KKR is far from overpaying. And it will also have management thoroughly on board through its new equity interests. The baton now passes to Sedgwick either to show it can, after all, create shareholder value in the public arena, or find a similarly satisfactory exit.

The transaction closed on 10 November 1998 and Willis left the public markets and became a KKR portfolio company.

Industry Mergers

Within two weeks of the announcement of the Willis/KKR deal Sedgwick had succumbed to a takeover offer from Marsh, and another famous name was consigned to history. This left three global firms, down from six only three years earlier. Few industry observers would have expected Willis to have been one of those left standing.

CHAPTER THIRTEEN

KKR and the IPO

Once the deal had been completed, the non-executive Directors left the Board. Senior KKR representatives in the persons of Perry Golkin, Todd Fisher, Scott Nuttall and Jim Fisher (no relation to Todd) became actively involved in the management of the business. They brought a more rigorous and dispassionate approach, demanding accountability, strict cost control and fact-based decision-making. Being a private company enabled Willis to continue and accelerate the change programme out of the public gaze. As well as the costs associated with this there was continuing investment in the business from 1998 to 2000, notably building reinsurance operations in the United States and Europe and acquiring and increasing interests needed to expand the global network in Germany, Norway, Argentina, Colombia, Mexico and Venezuela. There was an increasing focus on the name 'Willis', and as part of the brand recognition initiative the firm changed its name to Willis Group Limited on 1 October 1999.

John Reeve agreed a five-year contract with the Board when he joined, and he completed this almost to the day. His greatest achievement was undoubtedly ensuring the continuing independence of Willis, enabling it to be one of the few remaining global brokers. Joe Plumeri succeeded him as Chairman and Chief Executive Officer on 15 October 2000, becoming the first non-British Chairman. It was chance that led to his appoint-

Joe Plumeri

ment. In June 2000, having retired from Citigroup, he was in Paris to watch the French Tennis Championships where he bumped into his old friend Mark McCormack, the sports agent particularly associated with tennis and golf. Their conversation led to a call from Henry Kravis of KKR asking him to go to London and meet John Reeve.

Joseph J. Plumeri (1943–) was born in Trenton, New Jersey, and attended Trenton Catholic Academy and Bordentown Military Academy. He then studied at the College of William & Mary and followed this by enrolling at New York Law School. In 1968 he joined the 40-strong stockbroking firm Carter, Berlind & Weill. The Weill was Sandy Weill. Prior to joining Willis Plumert had a 32-year career at Citigroup and its predecessor companies. As CEO of Citibank North America he led the integration of the consumer business at Citicorp and Travelers Group. He also served as Chairman and CEO of Travelers Primerica Financial Services, Vice-Chairman of the Travelers Group and President and Managing Partner of Shearson Lehman Brothers.

He was greatly taken by both the outstanding talent he found at Willis and the enormous dedication and commitment of people there determined to return the firm to its pre-eminent position. Possessed of a dynamic and extrovert style not previously witnessed at Willis, he reorganised management responsibilities, implemented stronger expense controls and put greater emphasis upon sales. Further investment was made in the global network, and the service company in Mumbai was greatly expanded. Revenue in 2000 was £861 million and profit before tax £129 million. High levels of interest on debt were largely offset by there no longer being dividend payments to shareholders.

In February 2001 Willis Group Holdings Limited was incorporated in order to re-domicile the firm from the United Kingdom to Bermuda. This avoided the cost of stamp duty on share transactions that would otherwise have been payable after the company went public again. In the same month, Bradstock's was acquired and merged with the Willis business in Australia. Also in 2001 the 51 per cent interest of Willis National was sold, as was PENCO, the North American wholesale business.

In June 2001 Willis again became a public company through an Initial Public Offering. Twenty million new shares (neither KKR nor any other shareholder sold stock in this offering) were offered and taken up at a price of $13.50. The price indication during the roadshow was given as $8 to $10 but the demand was so great – it was forty-four times oversubscribed – that the offer was priced at $13.50. In fact, on the opening day, the demand and supply did not broadly balance for some twenty minutes or so and the opening purchase was made by Joe Plumeri at $16.50. The shares were listed on the New York Stock Exchange under the symbol WSH. The proceeds from the sale were used to redeem the preference shareholdings of the six insurance companies who had supported the leveraged buyout three years earlier. Over the next few years debt was paid down and a succession of secondary offerings was made. KKR progressively sold their holdings, eventually exiting what had become one of the most successful investments in their history.

Total revenues in 2001 were $1.424 billion and operating income was $161 million. The firm by then had around 13,000 employees in 80 offices around the world.

Postscript

Looking back on a long and fascinating history, it is possible to discern the key events which shaped the firm. The 1898 merger of Henry Willis & Company with Faber Brothers forged their pre-eminent position in marine insurance; the 1929 merger with Dumas & Wylie served to reinforce this. Although the merger with Corroon & Black in 1990 severed the near century-old relationship with Johnson & Higgins, it enabled the firm to develop and expand unhindered by the ties it had created and it went on to produce what Willis had long cherished: a significant presence in the United States. Being taken private by KKR in 1998 ensured its independence.

In the decade since its refloatation as a public company the business has continued to prosper and grow under Joe Plumeri's leadership. The largest transaction was in 2008 when Willis acquired Hilb Rogal & Hobbs, at the time the eighth-largest insurance broker in the United States. The price paid was $2.1 million. Old family names were resurrected when the London market wholesale broking business was styled as Faber & Dumas Ltd. In 2010 revenue was $2.3 billion and net income $455 million. There were 20,000 employees, 3,000 of whom were in associated companies, and 400 offices in over a hundred countries.

The Willis Building in Lime Street is a mere five minutes' walk from Threadneedle Street where Henry Willis founded the business. Almost two hundred years on, the proud name of Willis endures.

Acknowledgements

In writing this book I have been greatly helped and encouraged by friends and former colleagues at Willis. Many have given hours of their time assisting me with the research and I would make special mention of four Chairmen of Willis, namely David Palmer, Roger Elliott, John Reeve and Joe Plumeri.

Particular thanks are due to Ian Macalpine-Leny, Peter Ledger, Terry Pey and Mike Etches, who reviewed early drafts and made many helpful and constructive suggestions, and to Peter Stevens and Christine Douse, who provided a great deal of valuable research material. I would also like to thank Adam Willis for a number of family photographs; Nick Taylor for the copy of the speech he gave at his father's Service of Thanksgiving, and the family of Edward Gumbel, who provided me with their father's unpublished memoirs. Ellie Round uncomplainingly typed and re-typed the manuscript over many months and Barbara Clifford did a wonderful job in restoring many old photographs. Roger Hudson at Haggerston Press was immensely patient with this first-time author and was tolerant of my frequent time delays. Any errors or omissions in the book are of course mine alone.

Sources

Richard Blodgett, *Johnson & Higgins: The First 150 Years*, 1993

Peter Bowring, *The Last Minute*, 2000

W. H. La Boyteaux, *Johnson & Higgins 1845–1945*, 1945

Digby Brindle-Wood-Williams, *Firm Foundations: The Origins of Willis Faber, 1828–1928*, unpublished

Henry Dumas, *The Dumas Family and Dumas & Wylie*, 1992

D. E. W. Gibb, *Lloyd's of London*, 1957

Edward Gumbel, *Recollections of my Personal Life*, 1996

Edward Gumbel, *Recollections of my Business Life*, unpublished

Godfrey Hodgson, *Lloyd's of London: A Reputation at Risk*, 1987

David Keir, *The Bowring Story*, 1962

Ian Macalpine-Leny, *UNISON – the Envy of its Competitors*, 2004

Robert Peett, *Covering the Skies: A history of Willis Corroon Aerospace*, 1998

John Prentice, *The Business and Battlecry*, 1991

Adam Raphael, *Ultimate Risk*, 1994

Margaret Reis, *The Secondary Banking Crisis 1973–75*, 1982

Edwin John Spencer, *Recollections of my Business Life*, 1925

Willis Faber Printing Services, *Review: house magazine of Willis Faber*, 1970–95

A. G. Wrightson, *Irons in the Fire: A record of the Matthews Wrightson Group of Companies 1901–1951*

Willis Annual Reports 1967–2001

Various legal documents relating to the mergers with both Stewart Wrightson and Corroon & Black and to the offer by KKR to acquire Willis Corroon